Praise for *The Ed Branding Book*

MW01134751

"As a seasoned lead
immense value of *The*
and Lynette White. T
striving to make a meaningful impact in the fast-evolving
landscape of educational leadership. It brilliantly encapsulates
the essence of branding and social influence in an educational
context, offering practical, insightful strategies that resonate
deeply with my experiences and beliefs in educational innovation. This book is not just a read; it's a journey toward transformative leadership in education."

—Jerry Almendarez, superintendent

"Share your story and change the world! There is tremendous
power in sharing our stories. Branding and marketing are
compelling ways to communicate who you are and what you
value as a person or organization. Dr. Bryant and Ms. White
have written a book that walks us through the *why* and *how* of
branding. In a time when public education is bombarded with
challenges, this book is an essential and valuable resource for
all of us."

—Dr. Rosa Perez-Isiah, assistant superintendent,
author, presenter

"*The Ed Branding Book* is an outstanding book that should
be required for every leadership program and for every school
and district leader. The content that the authors provide is
about getting to know the essence of oneself in order to lead
with confidence, resilience, and advocacy for the organization
one leads. The chapter on AI is phenomenal; both a tutor and
trainer on the topic with tips to guide the leadership work.
Truly a must-read!"

—Stacie Stanley, EdD, superintendent, coauthor
of *Leading while Female: A Culturally Proficient*
***Response for Gender Equity*, senior training associate**
at the Center for Culturally Proficient Educational
Practices, Zeta Phi Beta Sorority, Incorporated

"This is the book you never knew you needed. For all the people that never thought ed branding was a thing, this book is for you! Lynette White's mantra of 'tell your story' and Dr. Renae Bryant's empowering call to action to 'be a connecter' converge in a must-read guide that shares practical tips on how your brand should amplify your values and beliefs, which makes your communication most authentically you. The tips and strategies embedded in this book make it feel like your own personal workshop of how you can best shine a light on all the things going well in your space. When reading this book, I felt like I was in deep conversation with my 'girls' as they helped me take my communication to the next level. They accentuate the core principle that equity in education is about recognizing and addressing the unique needs, strengths, and cultural backgrounds of each student. Building your brand on this foundation ensures that all voices are not only heard but also valued. Dive into this transformative journey and watch your educational brand flourish."

—Dr. Nyree Clark, coordinator of equity and access, Colton Joint Unified School District

"*The Ed Branding Book* is an invaluable resource for educators at all levels. Dr. Bryant and Ms. White provide practical strategies that empower everyone from instructional assistants to superintendents to jump into self-branding and get out there and share their story. This book is a must-read for all of those truly invested in the productive future of public education. Finally, a book that is a real reflection of the unique challenge that is branding as an educator or educational institution! *The Ed Branding Book* is a practical guidebook filled with the cheat codes to successful educator branding and community engagement."

—Paige Boyd, elementary teacher

"In the world of school PR, Renae and Lynette's exploration of the why behind education, storytelling, and branding is both thought-provoking and inspiring. It has encouraged me to reflect on my own why in this field and reinforced the importance of owning our narratives to bring positive change to our educational communities."

—Christine Stephens, MBA, communications manager, Redlands Unified School District

"From novice to expert, if you are looking to empower others through your leadership skills and innovative ideas, *The Ed Branding Book* is a must-read! Bryant and White share their own personal social media journey but also equip readers with tips and tricks on how to start their own journey to make social media work for them. Reading this book will indeed help you level up your power to influence—personally and professionally!"

—Tiffany Hampton, director of student services

"Renae and Lynette don't just share why we should build our brands and tell our stories, they get to the how we can do it. From their personal examples to the frameworks and templates to do your own—everything is so accessible."

—Dr. Kimberly MacKinney, executive director, secondary schools, Fontana USD; ACSA Region 12 Women's Leadership Network Lead; chief counselor, ALA California Girls State

"This book is a game changer for school principals. It's a practical guide for mastering social media, crucial for showcasing a school's highlights. It goes beyond posting tips, emphasizing how to make it a meaningful experience. Importantly, it highlights the chance for leaders to deepen connections and tell their school's story innovatively. A must-read for navigating the demands of social media in education!"

—Lorena Rubio, elementary school principal, #CommunityBuilder

"*The Ed Branding Book* by Renae Bryant and Lynette White is a compelling read that depicts their life experiences intertwined into what defines their core values, magnifies courage, and builds relational capacity within them to be compelling change agents for education. Bryant and White humanize social media and traditional media as a transformational highway to influence and promote programs that edify scholars and those that provide a quality education. The lens they bring into focus to help scholars, colleagues, and the school community is compelling. Their step-by-step formula is comprehensible and precise. Their stories inspire me, their vision moves my soul, and their proven success is my cue as a call to action."

—Addie Ruiz, principal at Jefferson Elementary CNUSD

"*The Ed Branding Book* is an essential read for any educator looking to navigate the ever-evolving world of social media and creating a brand. Social media is not just a tool but a critical platform for connection between educators; this book brilliantly highlights the importance of an educator's presence online, as well as how to create a brand for others to follow. Lynette and Renae offer their personal stories of how social media and branding impacted their careers and provide insightful strategies for engaging with educational partners. They share practical tips and ideas to develop your brand through the use of a variety of social media platforms. This book is a must-read for any educator who aspires to harness the potential of social media to enhance their impact and foster a more connected professional learning and educational community."

—Dr. Kerri Braun, principal, SAUSD

"Educators are faced with more challenges than ever before. *The Ed Branding Book* provides administrators, teachers, and district leaders with a guide on how to change the narrative in public education and tools to connect and apply their core values to achieve positive relationships with those they serve. The authentic personal stories of Dr. Bryant and Ms. White are inspiring and motivating. These changemakers have provided leaders with a blueprint on how to amplify the positives that are happening in our schools every day."

**—Alison Bruner, assistant principal,
Anaheim Union High School District**

"As a school board member who is active on social media, I can tell you firsthand the power and importance of education branding. Telling the positive stories of public education is key for all of those who work in and around education, as well as those who benefit from it. *The Ed Branding Book* gives clear strategies for those who are hesitant to get on social media and those who are more experienced. In a time when incredible work is being done in public education, I highly recommend this book for educational staff and partners, as well as scholars and families."

—Mary Helen Ybarra, Corona-Norco Unified School Board member, 2024 CSBA School Board Member of the Year, California Association for Bilingual Education Board of Directors, director of legislative action

"Renae and Lynette's book is loaded with practical insight gained from experience and tailored for the field of K–12 education. Their emphasis on leading through storytelling and building community engagement should resonate with every school district. The examples, templates, and prompts they provide throughout the book will make it easy for even the most novice social media user to leverage different platforms to connect with their communities in a meaningful way. In a world where digital presence is paramount, *The Ed Branding Book* serves as a pragmatic and easy-to-read guide for school districts to harness the full potential of social media."

—Margarita Cuizon-Armelino, deputy executive director, Association of California School Administrators

"I wanted to share my excitement about *The Ed Branding Book*. Trust me, it's a game changer for the education space and beyond! Renae and Lynette understand the challenges educators face in building a unique brand and present practical strategies that are easy to implement. From creating a brand identity that reflects our core values to engaging with our audience authentically, this book is like having a sisterly guide to branding success. So grab a copy, and let's elevate our brands together!"

"Empower yourself, embrace your authenticity, and unleash the true potential of your personal brand with *The Ed Branding Book*. Great job, Dr. Renae Bryant and Lynette White."

"As the president of a public school educators union, one of my fundamental roles is to share the voices and stories of our members. Educators go above and beyond every single day for our students, but we do a terrible job of sharing our stories of the passion, love, and devotion we have for our students and their education. If you are like me and struggle trying to find the time or don't even know where to begin with creating a brand or sharing the story of your members, this book is for you. This book and the accompanying podcast are filled with real-world tips that you can immediately put to use to help you in your work to amplify your educator voice and, most importantly, advocate for your students."

"As an introvert who often shies away from sharing work-related posts on social media, *The Ed Branding Book* made me reflect on my brand, my why, my core values, and the fact that I should be posting about the work that I do as an educator because we do amazing work! *The Ed Branding Book* is written with the user in mind, with questions for readers to reflect upon, along with tips and strategies to assist educators on their own journey with their personal as well as organizational branding. Highly recommended for educators who want to learn how to showcase and promote their schools and programs!"

"This book is a must-have for school administrators! Branding allows school districts to present themselves to educational partners in a positive light. This counters the way that we in public education are often presented by the media and external groups. This book gives concrete tools on how we can tell our story to our constituents. I highly endorse this work."

—Dr. Mark E. Marshall, superintendent of Los Banos Unified School District

The Ed Branding Book

THE
ED
BRANDING
BOOK

HOW TO BUILD
EDUCATIONAL LEADERSHIP
WITH SOCIAL INFLUENCE

The Ed Branding Book: How to Build Educational Leadership with Social Influence
© 2024 Dr. Renae Bryant and Lynette White

This book is available at special discounts when purchased in quantity for educational purposes or for use as premiums, promotions, or fundraisers. For inquiries and details, contact the publisher at books@daveburgessconsulting.com.

This is a work of nonfiction; however, names, locations, personalities, and stories have been embellished or truncated to protect identities and to convey the essence of the incidents.

Published by Dave Burgess Consulting, Inc.
San Diego, CA
DaveBurgessConsulting.com

Library of Congress Control Number: 2024930574
Paperback ISBN: 978-1-956306-71-2
Ebook ISBN: 978-1-956306-72-9

Cover and interior design by Liz Schreiter
Edited and produced by Reading List Editorial
ReadingListEditorial.com

This book is dedicated to the heroes of public education: scholars, classified staff, certificated staff, administrators, superintendents, board members, families, and community partners. Thank you for the often quiet and invisible work you do. May this book empower you to harness the power of branding to illuminate the vital work you do daily, transforming education and lives one story at a time.

CONTENTS

FOREWORD
BY ADAM WELCOME

First off, YES to everything that Renae and Lynette have written in this book.

As I think back on my career working in school districts and having built my own business, which is completely reliant on me and my brand, here is what I think matters most: Social media platforms will come and go. Hashtags and even their relevance will change. The world will become noisier and more crowded, both in person and online. The videos you made two years ago may not make an impact like they used too. The why and how and what and when will, without a doubt, change.

But the one thing that will stay true is YOU. How you talk to people. How you treat people. How you care for all the people that you get to work with every single day.

And the way you can make the largest impact—an impact that will be sustainable beyond the bad news and crises that will inevitably come up—is to have conversations with people face-to-face. Make phone calls to people to both celebrate good news and also to deliver bad news. Take time to listen and talk, and even if no one's mind gets changed, at least the other person will know that you care.

Again, a resounding YES to all the ideas and examples and plans that Lynette and Renae and the other contributors have outlined in this very important book. Try everything they suggest, and do what works in your organization and for your brand. But make sure you're not just doing those things. Listen. Talk. Make calls. Visit with people. Surprise them with your listening and talking and calls and visits, and they will become the biggest advocates and followers of your brand!

INTRODUCTION

We live in what is called a VUCA world: one that is volatile, unpredictable, complex, and ambiguous. But futurist and author Bob Johansen challenges us to "flip the VUCA forces to terms that create possibilities and redefine VUCA as: vision, understanding, clarity, and agility." In this flipped VUCA model, communication is key to vision, understanding, clarity, and agility. Anyone in the world of education constantly finds themselves attempting to act with vision, understanding, clarity, and agility to help people navigate that which is volatile, unpredictable, complex, and ambiguous. And that is all a part of educational branding.

As scholars, staff, families, and communities face declining school enrollment, attacks on public education, book banning, challenges to social-emotional learning, the integration of more generative artificial intelligence, redefinitions of scholar success, and more, educational branding and leading with social influence has become paramount for any chance of success.[1]

---

1   L. Stanford, "What 2024 Will Bring for K–12 Policy: 5 Issues to Watch," Edweek, December 29, 2023, https://www.edweek.org/policy-politics/what-2024-will-bring-for-k-12-policy-5-issues-to-watch/2023/12.

Connections, stories, and relationships are the most important social currency when it comes to innovation. Branded people, sites, and organizations are able to influence others. The act of influencing reigns over that of directing, managing, or commanding. Influence inspires others to become a part of something. Educational branding is influence. Branding adds to the identity of an organization and makes people feel connected to it.

Walnut Valley Unified School District has over twenty thousand branded items. When you walk onto any campus, you'll see staff members wearing or carrying WVUSD branded shirts, sweatshirts, backpacks, journals, pens, and more. According to WVUSD Superintendent Dr. Robert Taylor, as part of this branding—and as a result of a connection one of the teachers has to the owner of the Vans company—WVUSD is giving away custom WVUSD Vans tennis shoes to every employee. The staff are proud of their district. They feel connected and eager to be associated with the brand. This creates greater community, a positive climate and culture—and influence.

In this "new normal" post-COVID world, the need for building positive climate, culture, and communication is at an all-time high. Your digital impression matters now more than ever, and a huge part of that is your brand identity. From Facebook to TikTok and everything in between, social media use is booming. Now more than ever, companies are maximizing their efforts to market to the masses utilizing its power, and the education world is beginning to follow suit.

The COVID-19 pandemic forced all of us to think outside the box in many ways, with figuring out new ways to communicate effectively and efficiently being at the forefront. Along with this, educators were forced to find ways to communicate with their communities and really meet them where they were. Enter social media! Social media became the preferred way to communicate vision, understanding, clarity, and agility. We had to connect. Educators everywhere scrambled to create profiles if they didn't already have them, so they could connect with their people quick, fast, and in a definite hurry! Those who already had an online presence had a leg up and were able to mobilize their communications efforts more efficiently.

So where does this tie into your brand? This book will touch on how we got here, years into the "postpandemic" era, when we are communicating via social media more than ever before. We will give you strategies to define your brand (vision, mission, and values), discuss the impact your brand or lack thereof has on your social influence in the communities you serve, and show how creating an online presence that is on-brand aids in your success as a leader. Branding yourself, your site, and your organization are three of the keys to being a successful leader. In this book, you will learn easy tips and tricks to get started, specific steps to embrace leading with social influence, and the benefits of dialing in your brand right now!

Renae Bryant's Education and Branding Why: Connection

Renae

My brand is "connection." This is more attributed to nurture than nature.

I was removed from my home by Child Protective Services when I was five. After I was returned to my mother, I attended a different school in a new city every year from kindergarten to seventh grade. So, I had to learn to connect with others quickly—and I did: When I was nine years old, I broke the record for most boxes of Campfire Girls candy sold, at 1,001 boxes. This was before the internet, so these boxes were sold standing in front of a grocery store and going door to door. I made a connection with each customer for every box of candy.

OVER 1,000 SALES FOR CAMPFIRE DRIVE

John Christian of Howard's Restaurant purchases the 1,001 box of Campfire Girls candy from Renae Bryant, breaking an all-time national record in sales for the annual drive.

The parents of Renae Bryant wish to express their appreciation to the citizens and businesses of Tuolumne County for their genreousity in backing Renae.

Special thanks go to "The 90's", "Howard's Restaurant" and "Foster's Freeze" for purchasing the last 30 boxes needed to put Renae over the goal of 1,000.

My biological father was a lot of things. He was handsome, intelligent, and charismatic. He was also a salesman, a hustler, and a grifter. My last memory of him is of him being placed into the back of a police car. Two years before that, he taught me how to talk to, connect with, and sell to strangers. Those skills delivered dividends in my high school years, when they helped teachers look past my punk rock teen angst and recommend me for scholarships and universities.

As a first-generation college student, my connection skills kept growing. Like many college students, I was in a band. Supporting that band required me to learn new connection-related skills, like branding, public relations, and promotions. I gained an obsession with branding and business books while in the entertainment industry, and it has never left me.

When I became an educator, I never expected that all of these skills—picked up from candy sales, hustlers, and punk rock shows—would be necessary. I quickly discovered I was wrong. From roles as bilingual instructional assistant to teacher to site administrator to district administrator to professor, I have constantly branded myself, my site, and my organization by telling positive stories of public education. Lifting the veil, creating greater transparency, and strengthening the connections between scholars, staff, parents, and community have become more and more important at every stage of my career.

Never was that more apparent than when I was tasked to lead the implementation of the first Vietnamese dual language immersion program in California at Westminster School District. All of the skills I learned in the entertainment industry were quickly put to use: from booking television appearances to pitching the *LA Times* to designing promotional materials, writing a marketing plan, and more. Instead of "Always be closing," my mottoes became "Always be branding" and "Always be promoting."

Public relations, promotions, and branding are all about connections. Connections are all about relationships, and nothing is more important than relationships. Since connections and relationships are the most important part of education, branding is braided in.

> Branding is important to a school district for sharing programs and opportunities with our community. It's especially important to appeal to our younger generation of parents.
>
> —MARY HELEN YBARRA, CORONA-NORCO UNIFIED SCHOOL BOARD MEMBER AND CALIFORNIA ASSOCIATION FOR BILINGUAL EDUCATION (CABE) DIRECTOR OF LEGISLATIVE AFFAIRS

Lynette White's Education and Branding Why: Storytelling

Lynette

My first role at a school district was as at a large urban high school, and boy, did I hit the ground running. During my time there, I was a jill-of-all trades: my roles included attendance technician, site clerk, registrar, and school office manager. I didn't know it at the time, but being a part of the team tasked with revamping this "bad" school's image was the first step toward what I do today.

I consider my brand to be "telling your story." A lot of people refer to me as the "tell your story girl," and I happily embrace the moniker. There is so much power in sharing your story, not only with your colleagues but with your students so they can see the varying paths to success that exist. Life isn't linear, but it can truly feel like all the successful people around you always knew EXACTLY what to do, when in fact that couldn't be further from the truth. From the first day I set foot on a high school campus as a staff member to the present day, where I have the joy of telling the stories of an entire school district, I've seen that brand and brand identity matter.

Leading with social influence has completely changed the trajectory of my career. My communications and social media journey began under the leadership of Superintendent Jerry Almendarez. You will be hard-pressed to find someone in educational leadership in California who doesn't know Jerry. (And if you don't know him, LOOK HIM UP NOW! Like right now.) He was one of the superintendents at the forefront of really utilizing the power of social media before COVID, which complemented his leadership style and reinforced his brand online.

Jerry tapped me to help him when he joined our district and he wanted to get his name and values out to the community quick, fast, and in a hurry! Time and time again we were told by members of the community how much they valued his transparency and for the first time they kinda understood what a superintendent does. This was January 2020, and we had no idea that by mobilizing our efforts on social media so quickly, we set into motion a level of transparency and trust that Jerry would need just two months later when schools needed to be closed for just "two weeks." Remember that?

Little did we know the longest two weeks of our lives were set to begin. I learned to pivot and adapt in record time. We still needed to show the good despite the constant bad. We got really creative on Zoom and with social distancing, but we continued to engage the community and because we had set up that trust and transparency consistently prior to the crisis, we had a little bit of trust that went a really long way. Did everything go perfectly? I'd be a liar if I said it did, but so many things were easier because the community trusted that the superintendent, cabinet, and board of education cared about them. Our transparency when telling the story of the district and its leaders paid off tenfold during the pandemic. And once the shock of what was really happening wore off, we continued to tell our story: the story of the staff rallying to support the community's needs, to support each other, and most of all to be transparent—even when that meant saying, "I don't know, but I will let you know when I do" (there was a lot of that during the pandemic, right?). We were given grace because we were transparent with the community.

A big part of the reason the community had trust in Jerry as the district leader was because they felt they knew him. This was amazing to hear, after all, our entire effort was to get the community to know his brand, what his values were, and to be transparent. I began to see the power of connecting with people not only in our community but also across the country and even the world.

> Consistency. A delivery cadence is critical to increasing readership. And content. Content. Content. With all communication on-brand.
>
> —ALLAN MUCERINO, SUPERINTENDENT AND PROFESSOR

So You Wanna Be a Podcaster?
The *Ed Branding Podcast*

Renae

In May 2020, I started the Leadership Book Chat (#Ldrshpbkchat) as a way to bring people together, provide free professional learning, and create a community where people could still make connections and expand their networks while isolated at home during the pandemic and #MeToo and Black Lives Matter movements. The authors of *Leading while Female* had started a private Facebook page. When I was invited, I then invited all the females I thought would want to be a part of this community. The Leadership Book Chat was born when I posted on that page, "We should have a book study." Dr. Delores Lindsey replied, "If you host it, we'll come." After *Leading while Female*, we had book studies for *How to Be an Antiracist* and then *The New Jim Crow, Ready for Anything, How Women Rise, Beyond Conversations about Race, The Unfinished Leader, Evolving Learner, She Leads, Leading Change through the Lens of Cultural Proficiency*, and *Lead with Collaboration*.

For Christmas 2020, I was given some podcasting equipment as a way to encourage me to start a podcast. Between the 24/7 demands of working in education during the pandemic and the Leadership Book Chat, my first thought was, "Ain't nobody got time for that!" Although I loved listening to podcasts and appearing on them as a guest, I could not wrap my head around how I could make time to host one myself.

"Just start. Because where you start is not where you're going to end up."

—ADAM WELCOME

Then I was invited on Adam Welcome's *The School District Podcast*. He generously gave me some very important advice when he told me that Lynette White and I had to start a podcast—yesterday! He was right.

Lynette

After Renae was interviewed by Adam Welcome for his podcast, she called me and basically said, "We need to do a podcast because Adam said so."

Good enough for me. The *Ed Branding Podcast* was born! Renae and I found our groove very quickly. We reached out to a few of our closest people and encouragers and were lucky to have everyone support our project by lending their voices to it. Podcasting, much like social media, is an incredible way to collaborate with people who you otherwise might never get the opportunity to meet. Working with educators from across the country has been an incredible experience. The connections we have made will last a lifetime, and we still get as excited for each episode as we did when we had no idea what this podcasting journey would have in store for us. As of this writing, the *Ed Branding Podcast* has been listened to in eighteen countries and fifty states! Never did we imagine the reach would be so great, but that's just part of the power of podcasting. It has the power to reach both near and far, and it can also be used to keep your community current on things going on within your district while providing the opportunity to amplify students' voices while teaching them some great skills. It's a tool that can do so much.

Branding: Now More than Ever

That's true of branding, too. Marketing and branding are incredibly powerful tools in education, and it's time we all learn to use them effectively. This book will show how classified employees, teachers, administrators, superintendents, and board members can embrace branding for the power of connection it has. It aims to demystify branding, public relations, and promotions for education. It's also a tool kit that will empower readers to amplify their stories for the benefit of themselves, their sites, and their organizations.

Now more than ever—in this time of attacks on public education, declining enrollment, and culture wars—we must own the narrative and become the media. Everyone who believes in the power of public education, and its role in strengthening and protecting our democracy, must do their part to share the stories of its successes. We have to do our part to make sure the public understands how incredible and necessary our public schools are and to counter the extreme narratives created by those who seek to destroy public education.

That's a big project, but even if don't think you know much about branding, it shouldn't be intimidating. Our approach to branding extends to your site, organization, community, and district, but it starts with you.

And you already have a brand—even if you don't think of it that way.

PART I

BRANDING YOURSELF

"Branding is not selling. Branding is building. And when you build something that people believe in and want to be a part of, it will last so much longer than if you're just building to sell."

—ADAM WELCOME, INTERNATIONAL KEYNOTE SPEAKER, AUTHOR, PODCASTER, FORMER PRINCIPAL, #KIDSDESERVEIT

1

THE IMPORTANCE OF YOUR BRAND

You have a brand. There. We said it. Let's just get that out of the way. Your brand is how you define and live out your core values on a daily basis. Your brand is also your purpose and the significance you want to make.

When your colleagues see your name, what do they think of? Are they coming to their own conclusions? Or have you established who you are and what your values are? If so, you've already got a brand. You don't have to explicitly spell out your brand in everything you do. But if you are intentional about how you put yourself out into the world consistently over time, it will be felt in all you do and say.

In this chapter, we will discuss the importance of branding for educators and how it can positively impact their careers and reputations. By cultivating and growing your branding as an educator, you can convey your own unique identity and a clear message about your values. This identity can help differentiate you from other educators. By creating a distinctive brand that is true to yourself, you will become known for the expertise you bring to the table. This brand recognition can lead to more opportunities for speaking engagements, collaborations, and other professional opportunities.

Another benefit of branding for educators is that it can help develop a community of supporters and advocates. By building a strong brand, educators can create a network of colleagues and other professionals who believe in their message and are willing to promote their work. This network can help educators reach a wider audience and build a strong reputation within the industry.

The best part about building your own brand is that you own it. The branding or marketing you might create for a school site or district remains there long after you've left (hopefully); however, YOUR brand goes with you. It will always set you apart from others.

Most of the educators we come into contact with say, "It's not about me, it's about my students/school/district." While that is true, it is *also* about you! You have earned the privilege to be a leader in whatever your role is. You are preparing for your future role. Whatever point you are at in your career, as a leader in your community, you need to start leading with social influence. That is not to say that you need a ton of social media posts with your face plastered all over them; however, there are many good reasons you should have a brand that is all your own.

> People often say, "You are what you eat." For me, the reality has been "You are what you do."
>
> I have built a personal brand around supporting innovation and helping develop the next generations of leaders. Our school district was one of the first in the country to go one-to-one with Chromebooks and Google Apps. We helped create legislation in the state of Illinois to introduce e-learning days instead of snow days. We created a project-based version of freshman year as a

school within a school model to reimagine teaching and learning.

Along with my friend and colleague Mike Lubelfeld, I host a monthly Twitter chat (#SuptChat) as a way to connect leaders around the country. We teach classes on the state and national level to support aspiring superintendents. We have written four books to help amplify amazing stories and encourage others.

Ultimately, my brand is nothing more and nothing less than the work we've been given the opportunity to do, and the amazing work of the educators I'm allowed to serve alongside every day.

—DR. NICK POLYAK, SUPERINTENDENT, AUTHOR,
COFOUNDER OF #SUPTCHAT

The Elements of a Brand: RED

Greg Creed and Ken Muench—of Yum! Brands and Collider fame and authors of *R.E.D. Marketing: The Three Ingredients of Leading Brands*— are the branding geniuses who helped Taco Bell rebrand. As a result of their work, the fast-food chain was even voted "best Mexican food in the United States" in a national survey. Now, we in Southern California will find that claim to be highly debatable, but that is the power of marketing and branding.

So, what do these legends consider to be the formula of successful branding? There are three components: relevance (cultural, functional, and social), ease (to notice and access), and distinctiveness (unique, ownable, and consistent).[2] Creed and Muench have rebranded Taco

---

2   G. Creed and K. Muench, *R.E.D Marketing: The Three Ingredients of Leading Brands* (New York, NY: HarperCollins, 2021).

"
Every interaction, in any form, is branding.

—SETH GODIN
"

Bell, KFC, and Pizza Hut with this approach. The RED approach to brand is what made these businesses popular again.

What about education? In a time of culture wars, board wars, declining enrollment, and twenty-four-hour easy access to news and media, branding for educators, sites, and organizations makes a difference. Defining your narrative and brand takes it one step further.

Your Brand Precedes You

Lynette

I'm the "tell your story girl." Renae is known in education circles as a "connecter" and a promoter of women. Because we've established these brands, people in the education world often know what we stand for even before they've met us in person.

A common misconception is that if you say you have a brand, you must be full of yourself or self-centered. This couldn't be further from the truth. Branding yourself is a way to set yourself apart from the herd by communicating your values and what you uniquely bring to the table. Your brand is your professional identity, and there is nothing wrong with owning that.

You have heard about "selling" yourself to the panel in a job interview, right? Well, think of a brand as how you separate yourself from the other candidates. If your brand precedes you—in a great way—before you enter that room, you will have the room in the palm of your hand. I can't tell you how many interview panels I have been on where I've heard things like, "Oh, wow, I know them because of their recent presentations," "I know their LinkedIn presence," and "I'm aware of them through a professional organization. I like that they do XYZ and show it."

The alternative is that the conversation goes like this:

"Did you check their socials?"

"Yeah. Nothing."

"OK. Well, let's see what they have to say."

Your brand introduces you before you even walk into that room. I recently experienced this when looking for a new role. First, I didn't have to do much looking because the brand I had established was already bringing potential employers my way. Next, when I did an interview, my brand preceded me so when my name was brought up, already people knew of me. Some had heard of or seen work I'd presented across the state of California. Others had been exposed to my strong social media presence. I quickly discovered that my name had entered rooms I hadn't even thought of entering yet. Even now after accepting my current role, I have prospective employers seeking out my expertise because the brand I have established is so strong.

One superintendent who has truly harnessed his brand is Terrence Davis. You can feel it in everything he writes and posts online, as you'll see in what he says here about how mindful he is of his brand.

In the realm of education, the beacon of courageous leadership illuminates a transformational path. Imagine a school or school district where leaders and students embody unwavering conviction, standing tall against the currents of conformity. That requires more than a label; my call to action for authenticity and strength in leadership is the phrase "courageous fire."

In a world where noise often drowns out one's inner voice and confidence, courageous leaders in education rise above. They champion what's right, not what's popular. They empower students, parents, and staff to embrace their truths and navigate the complexities of learning and resilience. The benefits ripple far and wide. The community witnesses living examples of ethical strength, learning that compliance is not the only choice. Parents entrust their children to leaders who prioritize principle over appeasement, creating a foundation of trust. Staff find inspiration in leaders who weather storms with grace, fostering a culture of innovation and growth.

"Courageous fire" emerged not from a mere whim but from the crucible of life's toughest decisions. It symbolizes the relentless pursuit of a better educational world—one defined by courage, honesty, and authenticity. "Courageous fire" is a legacy, a testament to an unwavering commitment to igniting minds and hearts unafraid to lead, unafraid to be right, and unafraid to be the difference.

—TERRENCE DAVIS, SUPERINTENDENT

How Do You Want People to Feel about You?

Lynette

One of the perks of being an executive assistant to a superintendent was being privy to conversations having to do with the hiring process. I cannot stress enough how many times I'd hear, "Have you checked their social media?"

The reality is your brand and social media presence can have a direct—good or bad—effect on your career and your ability to secure that next great position. Our brands and social media portfolios have helped both Renae and me secure positions, and we know they will continue to do so in the future. Anyone can easily look at our professional

"
Your brand is what people say about you when you are not in the room.

—JEFF BEZOS

"

social media profiles and see what we are about, what we value professionally, and what our storytelling looks like. This last part is especially important because a main part of my job is being the chief storyteller of the district I represent. When I am being hired, it's important for them to see what I can bring to the table. I can't tell you how many times people I met when I started my position were like, "I looked you up, love your work, and am so excited to have you on board." Lots of the staff members felt like they knew me and what I value already from seeing my brand.

Since we know that boards of education and executive cabinet members are already looking to see what your social influence looks like, give them something to see. Social media is your platform to really back up what that résumé says and what you say you can do in an interview. Your brand is pretty much a combination of what you value and what that makes others feel. Think about some of the brands you love. How do they make you feel? In the same way, when someone mentions you, for example, in a conversation, they feel a certain way. Let's dig even deeper: How do you want to make people feel when they think of your personal brand? When you start to think of your brand, think of what you value professionally. What is your passion? Do you love highlighting academic success? Is your focus on socioemotional health? Do you oversee activities? Take your passions and amplify them! There's nothing wrong with some humblebrag in service of being transparent and showing the things we do daily for the community we serve. But branding yourself is not like branding a product. It means communicating a set of values for what you represent professionally. Establishing a brand that is authentically you is the key.

Brand Inventory Activity

How are you embracing branding for all the benefits it holds?

1. What is your brand?
2. How is your brand amplified in the community you serve?
3. Is it current or dated?

4. Who was involved in defining the brand?
5. Does it meet the RED criteria (relevance, ease, distinctiveness)?

When people say your name, what are they going to think about? In 2010, I joined Twitter. That was the moment I realized I was not just building an online reputation but my brand.

We've all heard the word "brand" defined in so many different ways, and for me the simplest explanation is that a brand is your identifying mark. It's what people say or think about you when they say your name or talk about your organization. And what you do to build that brand is one of the most important aspects of your professional career. Here's my best advice on how to build your brand.

Be consistent: Don't sprint. Pace yourself and be consistent. Think about building a twenty-four-month runway to get started. It takes that long sometimes to get going, and consistency is key for others to learn about you and understand your brand.

Be simple: The simpler something is, the easier it is to remember and build upon. People can't remember complicated brands. Keep it simple.

Be memorable: There are a lot of people in the world building brands. Create a message that people will remember, and you will be memorable, too.

Be positive: There's too much negativity in the world already. Positivity always wins, always.

Be genuine: You need to believe what you're talking about. Your brand depends on it, and people will know if you're trying to fake it.

> You got this. I believe in you!
>
> —ADAM WELCOME, EDUCATOR, INTERNATIONAL
> KEYNOTE SPEAKER, AUTHOR, PODCASTER

Your Core Values

Renae

Brand is what people attribute to you, your site, department, and organization. When I was recruited to Anaheim Union High School District (AUHSD), it was a direct result of a connection I'd made with Superintendent Michael Matsuda. When I sat down for a ten-plus person conversation/interview, two of the panelists mentioned my social media presence and how I actively promoted Westminster School District scholars, staff, and community as well as all the work we were doing there. Posting about the great work done in the organizations I've been a part of has garnered more attention for them. The consistency of my storytelling has added value to the brand. When people feel comfortable with a brand, they align themselves with it.

In each podcast episode, we ask the question, "In one word or a short phrase, what would you say your brand is and why?" We were inspired to ask this question by Tara Martin, author and director of publishing at Dave Burgess Consulting, Inc. In one of our initial meetings with her, she started by saying, "My brand is 'be real.'" Then she explained why. After that, it was a no-brainer to ask that question of all of our guests. In fact, it's a great challenge for all individuals, sites, and organizations.

When discussing branding, storytelling, and social media, many people feel overwhelmed and don't know where to start. Well, it all starts with knowing your core values. Your brand is based on your core values. Since education is so purpose driven, it's especially important for educators to be able to define their own core values. I often wish that a teacher had led me in an activity to do so when I was younger. Some—like those of us who grew up in the church—may feel like those core values have already been defined for us, but it is important that we define and declare them for ourselves.

When you know your top five values, can define them simply, and state what they look like in action, leading and telling your story becomes much simplified. Any communication or branding you put out runs through the lens of your core values. From roles as a teacher, leader, and formal administrator, I have been asked to identify my core values many times. But once I defined them, they have not changed: love, courage, integrity, passion/purpose, and optimism/vision. What are your top five values?

Dr. Renae Bryant's Five Core Values
(Written in 2014 as a part of the University of La Verne Organizational Leadership Doctoral Program)

Value	What It Means to Me	Behaviors
#1 Love	Valuing love means to love myself and show love to others. It also means care of myself. Loving others means living by the Golden Rule and the Platinum Rule: Treat others the way they want to be treated.	The behaviors that I will show are: working out; eating healthy; taking time out for mental, physical, and spiritual growth; practicing the Golden and Platinum Rules; and encouraging the hearts of others.
#2 Integrity	Valuing integrity means being honest with myself and others.	Tell and live the truth.

#3 Optimism/ vision	Valuing optimism means staying positive with myself and others; always having a positive presupposition, remembering that you don't always know what another person is going through; having positive belief in my vision; and having the intention the vision will come to fruition.	Using only positive speech. Showing caring and understanding. Smiling. Showing positive energy.
#4 Passion/ purpose	Valuing passion and purpose means feeling strongly about what I am doing with my life and showing that in a positive way. Having a moral and ethical rationale for what I am doing.	Start with why. Lead with a story. Radiate passion in a positive, inspiring way.
#5 Courage	Valuing courage means doing the right thing when others choose not to. It means never allowing fear to control my words or actions. It means standing and speaking up for the oppressed.	The behaviors that demonstrate courage are right speech and actions, working for social justice and equity; and speaking my truth respectfully.

My top core value is "love." Since our core values determine our brand, it makes sense I prioritize relationships and that connection is the brand others attributed to me before I ever defined my brand for myself.

Core Values Activity

1. Reflect on your core values and write them out.
2. Select the top core value that represents your brand and lean into it.
3. Challenge yourself to find a symbol and a song that represent your brand. The symbol could be something you create or

write. It could be something you adopt that means something to you. Think of the song as your own walk-up music, like the songs baseball players pick to get them motivated as they get ready to bat.

4. Think of how you use social media. Do your posts reflect what your brand is? Can you explicitly amplify your brand?

_____ *Five Core Values*

Value	What It Means to Me	Behaviors
#1		
#2		
#3		
#4		
#5		

Your Own Personal Board

Who are the people you want to mentor and sponsor you in different areas of your life?

We call this group your own personal board of directors, and if you do not have one yet, you need to develop it. These should be people who have skills and talents that supplement your own. Take the opportunity to sit down with people you always wanted to have as mentors and ask them to be on your personal board of directors. Each person must be someone you can trust.

Once you have your personal board of directors, establish working agreements with them. These can be as simple as the four agreements discussed by Don Miguel Ruiz in his book by the same name or something more detailed and explicit.[3] This is a two-way relationship, so be clear and explicit in what expectations each of you have.

Now that your personal board of directors is established, calibrate your brand with them.

Personal Board of Directors Activity

- Think about where you can look for members of your personal board of directors. Consider:
    - Mentoring programs
    - Networking events
    - Your network
    - Reaching out to peers and colleagues
    - Professional associations
- Find a personal board of directors or advisory board worksheet that works for you, or make your own with questions like:
    - Who is an expert in the type of work you do?
    - Who has a position or role you would like to have one day?
    - Who would challenge you to act boldly?
    - Who would be a good branding or social media mentor?
    - Who could you count on for inspiration?
    - Who would be a good career counselor?

---

3 M. Ruiz and N. Wilton, *The Four Agreements: A Practical Guide to Personal Freedom* (San Rafael, CA: Amber-Allen, 2012).

PERSONAL BOARD OF DIRECTORS

	PERSONAL DIVISIONAL UNITS				
	Career	Leadership	Finance	Family	Spiritual Growth
Blog/Podcast					
Books					
Self-Study Course					
Conference					
Membership					
Coach					
Mentors (People)					

(Left axis label: BOARD MEMBERS)

J. D. Horst, EHS Daily Advisor, https://ehsdailyadvisor.blr.com/ 2020/01/your-personal-board-of-directors-go-beyond -mentorship-with-your-professional-development/, January 21, 2020.

Your Vision and Mission Statement

Renae

As you develop your brand and schedule your social media posting, how can you be sure your posts and message consistently align with your core values? Whether you're a classroom teacher, coordinator, or director, it's important to continually be reflecting on your purpose and the significance you are trying to make. As leaders (even when we're only leading ourselves), we need to be able to define our brand (core values) and significance (vision and mission).

In the entertainment industry, my brand was connection, just like it is now. My purpose and significance were centered on using the arts to amplify the rights of humans, women, children, LGBTQIA+ people, and environmental, animal, and social justice. My purpose now is grounded in designing systems and processes with scholars, families,

"**Significance isn't what we get . . . It's what we do for others.**

—SETH GODIN"

staff, and community to create greater access, equity, and success for these same scholars.

Schools and districts have vision and mission statements. What is your personal vision and mission statement? We asked you earlier to write out your core values. Now we are asking you to write your own personal vision and mission statement. Like the core values activity, this is an activity the University of La Verne had us complete in the first year of the doctoral program and an activity that I have my own first-year doctoral students complete each year.

Like with your core values, you should calibrate your mission and vision statement with your personal board of directors.

> Are you doing something powerful at work? It is your moral imperative to share your story or expertise. You have a moral imperative to get good at sharing that message.
>
> —DAVE BURGESS, AUTHOR, PODCASTER, SPEAKER, AND CONSULTANT

TIPS, STRATEGIES, AND REFLECTIONS

- Define your personal core values. What are the core values, mission, and vision of your site and/or organization? How can you leverage these in your storytelling and branding?

- What is your brand? Can you define it in one word?

- What steps do you take daily to cultivate that brand?

Please share your reflections using the #EdBranding hashtag and visit EdBranding.net for more ideas on branding yourself.

2

LEADING WITH SOCIAL INFLUENCE

Brand Influence

Leading with social influence! That has been the tagline I've used at presentations for the past few years, and it always attracts both interest and questions.

What makes an influencer? You are an influencer because you influence others.

You influence scholars, staff, families, and community members. Influence is the most sophisticated form of power. It is the ability to modify how a person develops, behaves, or thinks based on relationships and persuasion.[4] Your influence is not necessarily based on positional or hierarchical power but on your relationships and connections.

---

4   A. Botwin, "Power vs Influence: How It Can Make or Break Your Organization," SPC Consulting, October 3, 2022, https://www.strategypeopleculture.com/blog/power-vs-influence/.

> Social media branding is why I am now an author, speaker, and consultant. It has absolutely expanded and influenced my personal goals.
>
> —DR. ROSA PEREZ-ISIAH, ASSISTANT SUPERINTENDENT

Why You Should Be an Influencer

Lynette

What is leading with social influence? The technical definition of leading with social influence is any change in an individual's thoughts, feelings, or behaviors caused by other people—who may be actually present or whose presence is imagined, expected, or only implied. That's a mouthful, right? Well to sum it up, we, as educational leaders, are often the pillars of the community, site, or district we serve, and we have a certain level of influence through the things we do daily. My spin on leading with social influence is really mirroring what you'd like to see by influencing people positively by utilizing the power of social media. Social media is where our audience is. It is the one place where you can effectively contact your key educational partners, such as students, families, staff, and the community, as a whole and for free. Work smarter, not harder! If you already know where the people are, then half the battle is done.

It's one thing to say you're an awesome leader, but it's a very different thing to *show* how you're an awesome leader. Social media provides your community with an unobstructed view of what you do and what you value. Bonus points if you engage with the content, comment, like, and repost. All of that counts, and it shows your staff that you see them and that what they are doing has value. This goes for students, too.

And by utilizing the power of social media, you'll have the ability to have your finger on the pulse of the community. For example, a

"People really see the content being pushed out on my end. They have a good sense of my value system, and they have a good sense of the community I serve and how and why I make decisions."

—JERRY ALMENDAREZ

superintendent cannot be in all the places all the time, but by surfing through social media feeds and engaging with them, you can be aware of what's going on all around your district. Leading with social influence allows you to have a group who will lead as you do, and you—the busy superintendent—can see what's going on at your sites without leaving your office. Does this mean no more site visits? Of course not, but it is one more great way to maintain that connection with your staff and sites.

lynettewhitesocial
Santa Ana Unified School District

...

View insights   Boost post

  Liked by **drrenaebryant** and **73 others**
lynettewhitesocial Happy Friday SAUSD! What sites are we headed to today? #WEareSAUSD #SAUSD #BetterTogether

Aside from that, by leading with social influence you will positively influence others around you to do the same, cultivating a community of storytellers. I always feel the more voices we have telling our stories the better. If you amplify each other and promote positivity, at the end of the day you will have a feed that is filled with your professional successes and the professional successes of those around you.

One of my favorite stories of the power of leading with social influence is from working with Dr. Frank Miranda. When I started working with Dr. Miranda, he had been superintendent for about two years and had dabbled in social media but never really leaned into it. He calls me his reverse mentor because I really helped him see the power of social media and the benefits it could bring him and the district as a whole. Eventually, Dr. Miranda slowly started using social media more frequently and utilized it to see into the school sites within the district. One day he saw a really awesome post from one of the teachers in the district. This teacher had students make presentations for Women's History Month, and the subsequent post really resonated with Dr. Miranda. He decided to pay the teacher and class a visit to compliment them on a job well done. The teacher was thrilled to see her post and her work being validated by the superintendent, and Dr. Miranda was able to recognize a few students from the post and compliment them individually. The look on the students' faces was just wonderful. *This* is why leading with social influence is so important. Now I know there will be people who will say, "OK, but it's still *just* social media." Yes it is, but to the students and teacher that day, they felt seen by someone in a position of power and validated for what they had done. Dr. Miranda felt great, too. Social influence had given him an opening that he otherwise wouldn't have had to connect with the students and teacher.

I have successfully created and implemented a brand ambassador program in two districts in Southern California on the basis of leading with social influence. Most of you have heard about brand ambassadors for everything from clothing to supplements: they are basically people who vouch for a brand and are usually compensated for it. Well, I decided to take the idea and apply it to education. After all, at the end of the day, the best cheerleaders for our sites and districts are our staff members. Anyone who knows me knows this is near and dear to my heart. It's OK if I'm the only person telling the district's story, but it also makes for a one-sided version of the story. Brand ambassadors help tell a complete story of a site or district. After all, we can't be in all places at all times—unless we have some help. It takes a village, right? Well, I start building that village by asking for volunteers who would like to tell the story of their site or department. I support them along the way by providing help with content creation and professional development so they can feel confident in telling their own story.

Besides building a community of storytellers, I am also building capacity in our staff, forming relationships, and helping them lead with social influence. Brand ambassadors can be anyone from the nutrition services worker to the superintendent. The purpose of working with such a broad range of people is equity. Everyone has a seat at the table of storytelling. It's also helpful for the busy principal who doesn't have time to tell the story of their site but does have an eager teacher who loves documenting the awesome project he is doing with his class. By recruiting these volunteers, we are ensuring that a robust story of the district is told. Having a communications department is great, but even if you don't, creating a deep bench of storytellers for your community is doable. It also creates a greater sense of belonging in the staff. Besides, we all have our phones on us all the time—let's use them for something good! Leading with social influence is so much more than social media: it helps build relationships across your organization and beyond.

lynettewhitesocial
Santa Ana Unified School District

...

View insights

Boost post

    Liked by **thewrightleader** and **53 others**

lynettewhitesocial We are so excited to launch our new SAUSD Brand Ambassador program!! We will be having an informational meeting this Friday at 11am via Zoom... more

---

Branding in education and social media has changed so much for me as a classroom teacher. I love the connectivity with my classroom, my district, and my community. Getting involved in the brand ambassador program for my district and social media has only created positive opportunities for me and my school.

—PAIGE BOYD, ELEMENTARY TEACHER

Brand can also be a feeling of authenticity, transparency, and trust within the community you serve. It definitely requires a mindset shift to see that by leading with social influence, you are not being self-serving but actually being an accessible leader in your district, one who spreads the word about the wonderful work being done on your campuses. Part of our jobs in education is to share the stories of our successes with the community. We must stop hiding what we do well.

lynettewhitesocial

•••

View insights

Boost post

Liked by jerryalmendarez and **49 others**
lynettewhitesocial Super fun morning w/ @drkerribraun presenting about stakeholder social media engagement! Thank you @cueinc for the opportunity, ready to take... more

By being your true authentic self on social media and showing the things you value professionally, you will be front-loading all the positivity possible so when that inevitable "bad thing" happens, you will have community buy-in, trust, and established relationships to assist you in getting through it. George Couros said something that sums up my social media style: "We need to make the positive so loud that the negative is almost impossible to hear."[5] If you've flooded the platform with positive stories, then the negative won't be the only thing people remember. So flood those channels with all the good stuff going on! So often we dwell on what's going wrong, but there's a ton of things going right, too. Our job as leaders is to show it. Highlight student and staff achievements, welcome new staff members, and celebrate the diversity within your district that allows us to learn from each other.

Know Your Values

Renae

As the world and organizations become more "flat," we are all sharing stories and connecting at an even greater speed. Your story and ability to convey it is your brand. Your brand is your connection. Your connections are your relationships. We know that nothing is more important than relationships. What all that means is that, for educators, branding yourself, your site, and your organization is no longer optional.

We all have a *why* for education. What is our why for leadership in storytelling and branding? My core why is about owning the narrative. In a sea of negative stories about public education, it's crucial to lift the veil and pump out as many positive stories and images as possible to highlight the great work of public education.

My own journey has demonstrated the power of storytelling and branding for educators. In fact, promoting and branding via social media probably saved me professionally. Do tell, you say. OK.

Well, as the first coordinator of English learner (EL) programs at Westminster School District (WSD), I was hired to not only increase

---

5   G. Couros, *The Innovator's Mindset* (San Diego, CA: Dave Burgess Consulting, Inc., 2015).

the equity, access, and success of EL/plurilingual scholars in the district, but specifically to roll out the first Vietnamese dual language immersion (DLI) program in California. I was told that this program was ten years in the making and we would have fifty to one hundred families at the first Vietnamese DLI family information night we hosted. Let's just say that was not a realistic projection. We had three families attend the first information night.

I could tell my new superintendent was worried. She followed me back to my office that night, where she told me, "This has to be successful." I asked her not to worry and told her that now that I knew it was going to take some serious "street team" efforts, I would get busy. "I promise I will fill two classes," I told her and then prayed all the way home that I could make it a reality. She called me into her office the next week and said, "I know you are in your doctorate program right now. It is imperative we successfully implement Vietnamese DLI. You will work on your dissertation on your vacations. For now, your nights and weekends are mine." Needing my job, I said, "Yes, ma'am."

The next day I started an implementation and promotional plan. I met with the DLI Task Force and asked them for their input. Where should I promote? How should I promote? Who was willing to help me promote? What should I know about the Vietnamese community that might make promoting and marketing to them different from another audience? Who could be allies in the community? Who were the influencers? Who did I need to become friends with or connect with? Who did I need to get in front of and talk about the program? What Vietnamese radio, television, and newspapers were available to do a feature on the program? What groups in the community did I need to partner with? Who wanted to see the first Vietnamese DLI program in California succeed? How could I make my promotional efforts visible and transparent?

I knew this plan would have to involve social media. Even though I had one of two bosses who wanted to see the program fail (because they wanted the new superintendent to fail), I knew I had at least one ally in Dr. Natalie Tran, CSUF professor and director of the National

Resource Center for Asian Languages. She is Vietnamese and was my friend on social media. So, I went through Dr. Tran's Facebook friends and started friending any that I thought might like to know about the first Vietnamese DLI program in California. I tagged her and the new Facebook friends I garnered in my posts about the program. I asked Dr. Tran to connect me to the Vietnamese American Chamber of Commerce (VACOC). This led to me hosting the VACOC at the district for the monthly meeting and presenting to them about the program. They featured the flyer in their online newsletter. I also added any WSD employee and community member (including board members) I could find on social media. I wanted us to get to know each other better, but I also wanted everyone to see where I was on what day promoting the district and the program.

I was told to promote the program at the weekend Vietnamese language and culture school, so I stood at the door of the school like it was the exit at a musical venue and passed out hundreds of flyers for the program. I appeared with Dr. Tran and members of the community on any Vietnamese television and radio that would host us. Even though I had a colleague who told me I would be "lucky to fill one class" and that I "should stop promoting the program when I hit the number fifteen," I attended and promoted at the Fall Festival Tết Trung Thu, Lunar New Year Tết Parade, and OC Tết Festival, following families with small children around giving them flyers. I drove all over Orange County (OC), leaving flyers at preschools and Vietnamese grocery stores and libraries. I drove in every weekend, dedicating half of every Saturday to promotion. I even placed brochures and flyers on the windshields of cars at the Asian Garden Mall off Bolsa (an area considered the Little Saigon of Orange County). We hosted night, weekend, and weekday parent-information meetings.

I kept promoting, and as I promoted, I took photos and posted them on social media with captions like, "Proud to promote the first Vietnamese Dual Language Immersion Program in California at Westminster School District." I started the WSD Office of Language

Acquisition Facebook and Twitter pages, documenting all the efforts on my personal and professional pages. Whenever we had our DLI Task Force meetings, I included photos of my promotional efforts. I updated them on the DLI enrollment numbers. I was asked to update the board on our efforts.

And, little by little, we filled two classes.

Using social media to document my efforts, I went from fearing the loss of my job to promoting the program to being promoted to executive director and being able to build the first office of language acquisition at the district made famous by the 1947 *Mendez, et al. v. Westminster School District* case, which ended segregation in California and set the precedent for *Brown v. Board of Education* in 1954. We went from hosting three families at a time at family information meetings and barely filling two classes to filling three kindergarten classes. We went from begging Vietnamese media to feature us to being featured in the *Los Angeles Times*, *OC Register*, *Education Week*, New America, the Education Trust–West, and National Public Radio. I went from calling mentors worried about my professional situation to being awarded 2017 OCDE Countywide English Learner Advocate of the Year, earning my doctorate in three years, being called by AUHSD Superintendent Michael Matsuda, and recruited to serve and implement the first secondary Vietnamese DLI program in the United States. Before leaving WSD, I wrote the Barona Indian Group Grant for $5,000, which was awarded to the school site by State Senator Janet Nguyen. I also wrote the California School Board Association Golden Bell Award nomination, which was won as I started my role at AUHSD. Then I used all the experience and knowledge garnered from storytelling, branding, and connecting at WSD to successfully launch the first secondary Vietnamese DLI program in the United States at Magnolia High School.

In *BrandED*, Eric Sheninger and Trish Rubin identify a district's brand as composed of its image, promise, and result. School districts must be purposeful in how information is disseminated to build a brand. Effectively branding information is beneficial to a district internally in times of contentious negotiations and externally as it fights declining enrollment. An individual educator's brand is established through developing and telling the story of the district.[6] If you do not tell your own story, it will be told for you. And so I've told my story to show that with the increase of communication through the internet and social media, it is important that classified employees, teachers,

6   E. Sheninger and T. Rubin, *BrandED* (San Francisco, CA: Jossey-Bass, 2017).

administrators, superintendents, board members, colleges, universities, families, and community partners embrace branding and storytelling for the power of connection it has.

"Evolving." As an educator, author, and speaker, I'm in love with this word! The only constant in my career (ahem, my life) is change, and "evolving" represents the purposeful pursuit of improvement over time. It's about building upon our strengths and striving for growth.

My favorite Dylan Wiliam quote is, "If we create a culture where every teacher believes they need to improve, not because they are not good enough but because they can be even better, there is no limit to what we can achieve." To me, this is evolving. This is what I want to do, and this is what I want to help others do.

Evolving serves as the guiding principle for my work. I'm advocating for continuous improvement through positive relationships, and I do this by focusing on:
- Bringing communities together and cultivating a sense of belonging
- Promoting growth (socially, emotionally, behaviorally, academically)
- Honoring and celebrating what makes each of us unique and dynamic

My brand is an evolving journey focused on personal and professional flourishing. With an emphasis on connection and growth, I empower individuals to become their best selves and make a positive impact in the world. Together, we can evolve!

—LAINIE ROWELL, AUTHOR, KEYNOTER, AND CONSULTANT

TIPS, STRATEGIES, AND REFLECTIONS

- Define your why for storytelling and branding in education. Why does it matter to you, your site, and/or organization?

- What story needs to be told and why?

- Make your storytelling and branding visible on social media and be unapologetic about it.

- Who are or could be your brand ambassadors? How will you empower them to tell the story? How can you gamify your brand ambassador program?

- How do YOU lead with social influence?

Please share your reflections using the #EdBranding hashtag and visit EdBranding.net for more ideas on leading with social influence.

3

WHICH PLATFORM AND WHY?

Most of us will not pop onto the social media scene and immediately engage with thousands of people. The most important thing is just to choose a platform, start using it, and calendar time to engage, even if it's only for fifteen minutes a day. Superintendent Joe Sanfelippo is a great example of making the most of your time with his walking and recording leadership reflections then posting on social media. As Dave Burgess said, "We have a moral imperative to share our story."

But how do we start?

Lurk!

Renae

I joined MySpace back in the day. I joined Facebook in 2008 and established a professional account in 2012, which is now my personal and professional account. I joined Twitter (now X) earlier than many. I really opened the account to share the awesome things we were doing in the classroom. The name of my account then was "MsBryantsClass." No joke. The same thing happened with Instagram. I started a LinkedIn account around the same time. Around that time, I had the same thought many of you have: "How am I going to keep up with all of this? Please don't develop another platform!"

Well, they did. And to keep up with all of it, I did exactly what I am now advising others to do: lurk.

I was an earlier adopter to some platforms because I had reverse mentors telling me which ones to join. Before I was at Westminster School District, I spent fourteen years at Corona-Norco Unified School District. There, I worked with Dr. April Moore, an amazing leader who was one of the first women to earn her doctorate at the district (and the first to host a *Lean In* book study in the Inland Empire). She was really savvy about technology, and she was also one of the first female educators I knew on Twitter. I followed her there, and then I followed some of the people she followed.

Dr. Moore was also the person who told me I could attend the Association of California School Administrators as an aspiring administrator. When I saw Eric Sheninger speak about embracing technology, MOOCs, BYOD, and social media use at the Association of California School Administrators New and Aspiring Principals Academy at UCLA, I felt validated. I also looked at who Eric followed online, and I started following those educators.

Eventually, I scheduled time on my calendar to post. Even if it wasn't at the optimal time, I just posted. It became a digital portfolio of my professional work. Education is my passion and purpose, so it was easy. I felt as though I was adding value to the profession by sharing.

Honestly, leveraging social media and branding is a struggle for me—I'm uncomfortable with self-promotion and "selling" my work.

My best tip is to be attentive to what you find compelling in other educators' social media posts and try to integrate those into your own work. For example, I love seeing posts that show groups of educators using books (at conferences, professional learning sessions, etc.), selfies with the author, photos, or Google slides with annotated pages from books, "what I'm reading" posts, and blog posts where readers talk about what they learned or implemented from a book. I take note of these and try to find ways to incorporate them into my own posts.

My other tip is to follow other educators and scholars who do social media well! @DrRenaeBryant, @AlyssaDunn618, @ProfHsieh, and @ValentinaESL are on my short list of scholars to watch!

—DR. ALISON DOVER, PROFESSOR AND AUTHOR

So, which Platform?

OK, let's get into some data for the people who need it. Why do educators in particular use social media?

- 81 percent of educators use social media to get inspired with new teaching ideas.
- 54 percent connect with other educators.[7]

This shows that educators have seen the value in collaborating on social media. They seek it out. But where do you start?

---

7   University of the People, "Teachers and Social Media: The Online Pros and Cons," December 20, 2022, https://www.uopeople.edu/blog/teachers-and-social-media/.

"Having a platform to be able to lift the voices of others is so important.

—JESSICA GOMEZ"

LinkedIn

It might seem that LinkedIn is for job seekers only, but you can think of it is as a more professionally dialed-in Twitter (X). LinkedIn is a platform specifically designed for professionals to connect with others in their industry. Having a strong presence on LinkedIn can enhance an educational leader's personal brand and visibility within the industry. It allows them to showcase their achievements, highlight their contributions to the field, and demonstrate their passion for education.

You'll find an abundance of professionals on LinkedIn, and the format scrolls like social media. Your followers here are really based on your professional network and should be related to your current employer, the schools you attended, and topics are aligned with your profession. LinkedIn is an excellent platform for educational leaders to showcase their expertise, accomplishments, and experience. Doing so can attract the attention of recruiters and educational institutions looking for talented leaders to fill positions or participate in advisory roles. A LinkedIn profile page reads like your résumé with additional spaces to add in what you excel at. People can even endorse the skills you list. It's the ultimate place to display your brand, keep it fresh and relevant, and connect with a wonderful professional learning network. It can even help you find that next amazing role you've dreamed of.

LinkedIn is a great platform for connecting with exactly who or what you need. Overall, LinkedIn provides a professional platform that allows educational leaders to leverage their expertise, grow their network, and stay informed about the developments in the education industry. It serves as a digital hub for education professionals to connect, collaborate, and advance their careers.

Twitter (X)

Twitter (X) offers educators a unique platform for professional development, networking, sharing resources, and staying updated on educational trends. It connects educators worldwide, providing a unique opportunity to gain insights into different educational systems, cultures, and practices. This is where your people are. Meet them there and collaborate with each other. It's a platform that allows educators to build a diverse and extensive network of other educators, administrators, and experts from around the world. This network becomes a valuable source of ideas, inspiration, and support. By following educational thought leaders, attending Twitter (X) chats, and participating in education-related discussions, educators can access a wide range of professional development opportunities in real time.

Both of us have personally found our PLNs (professional learning networks) on Twitter (X). The education folk who excite and inspire us are there. The education community on Twitter (X) is great and incredibly giving of their time and expertise. Twitter (X) hashtags related to education (#SuptChat, #EdTech, #EdBranding, #SchoolPR) facilitate focused discussions on specific topics. Educators can join these conversations to exchange ideas and learn from others in their field.

This is a platform where you definitely need to have a professional account; it is way too easy to fall into the hole of politics, pop culture, feuds, and trolls. Keep that account professional and aligned to your values—aligned to your *brand*. Your Twitter (X) account should be seen as a portfolio of sorts, a place where districts and other educators can see what you are all about. They can see your version of storytelling, and they should be able to feel your brand all over the page.

Students have already found their way to this platform, because being as innovative and smart as they are, they quickly determined that this is where college coaches spend their time. Twitter (X) is where students are marketing themselves, and a lot can be learned from this. Lynette's son and his friends, for example, contact coaches, post videos, and tell their stories on there because they've found their captive audience (coaches!). The college coaches she has spoken with say this helps them because the content is easily accessible and comes to them directly. Students using the power of social media to market their own brand—we can all learn from this!

> I've been a Twitter user since 2010, and with Twitter, I have been able to establish a positive, professional brand in three superintendent posts. In addition, I use LinkedIn, Facebook, Instagram, podcasting, video, and other social media to get the messaging out about my district as well as my roles as a superintendent, a leadership developer, and an author. How has it positively shaped all of this? IMMENSELY—the reach, the connections, the global communication "flattening," all of the above! It's been essential.
>
> —DR. MICHAEL LUBELFELD, SUPERINTENDENT, AUTHOR, PODCASTER, COFOUNDER OF #SUPTCHAT

Facebook

By having a presence on Facebook, leaders, sites, and districts can establish a controlled, professional public presence that maximizes influence in the most popular social media space in the world. Your community loves Facebook. It is where your parents and teachers are. Being active on this platform allows your organization to be in control of the narrative and really guide the story of the organization in a place where the people are. There's a reason people say, "If it happens on Facebook, it must be true!"

Facebook Live is a cool and easy way to engage with your community, particularly working parents. Facebook Live really took off during the pandemic, and it is one of the most commonly asked about items when it comes to schools and districts being on social media. Families loved the ability to log onto Facebook Live to see events at the school they can't attend. It's an easy way to ensure that all families have access to what is going on at their child's school or district even when they can't be physically present.

This is the platform leaders and organizations should be on to keep a finger on the pulse of the community as a whole. Full transparency: There is a good and a bad side to Facebook. Community groups are common on this platform. Join them if you want to be informed about the community you serve; however, be aware that these tell the good, the bad, and the ugly from the point of view of whoever is posting. You will have to use your strength to not engage. On the flip side, it's better to be aware of the buzz going on about the district than to be blindsided. At least if you know the buzz, you know possible areas for improvement.

Instagram

Instagram is what we will call the triple threat of social media. This platform allows you to connect with not only families but also students and staff. There are more and more educators on Instagram every day, so the collaboration with fellow educators is beginning to rival Twitter (X). It gets to the community as a whole.

Instagram is by far one of the most popular platforms. As far as engaging more members of your community goes, it's worth looking for the best return on investment (ROI) on the time you spend crafting posts. The ROI on Instagram is tremendous in terms of the size and breadth of your audience.

That's especially true of Instagram stories and reels, which are where you should spend the most time on Instagram. It scrolls like TikTok, so the students love it, but it also allows you to see more content than just scrolling the feed. A great post can get several likes, but a great reel or story will easily triple that number, simply because it allows people to swipe and watch. This is the generation of now, so think about that when you post on Instagram. Add things to your feed but really *live* in the stories, where your content reach is much greater.

TikTok

TikTok is a social media platform for sharing short-form videos. If LinkedIn is the platform most geared toward professional networking and career development, TikTok allows educational leaders to showcase their personalities and human sides.

TikTok provides an opportunity for educational leaders to share content in an engaging, creative, and entertaining manner. You can create short educational videos with tips or fun challenges related to learning, entertainment, and creativity. It's also great for motivating students and promoting educational initiatives. Educational leaders can use TikTok to raise awareness about important educational issues, such as mental health in schools or equity and inclusion. They can also advocate for causes and initiatives relevant to education. It's a good way to promote extracurricular activities, too, and educational leaders can use TikTok to showcase the achievements and talents of students and educators within their schools. This can help foster a positive school culture and boost morale in the school community.

By participating in trends, sharing personal experiences, or showing behind-the-scenes moments, educators can make themselves more relatable to the TikTok community. Being present on TikTok in a professional manner allows educational leaders to engage with a younger demographic and reach a wide audience of students, teachers, and parents. TikTok often reflects the interests, challenges, and trends of the younger generation. By being on the platform, educational leaders can gain insights into the current interests and concerns of students and adapt their approach accordingly.

It's important to note that while TikTok can be a useful platform for educational leaders to connect with a younger audience and promote education, it should be used thoughtfully and responsibly.

Content shared on TikTok should align with the values and objectives of the educational institution and should prioritize the well-being and privacy of students and staff.

> Social media has allowed me to share my experiences, highlight all areas of my leadership, and promote myself nationwide. Additionally, I have been able to connect with other educational leaders from around the nation. Social media has also allowed me to grow and improve in my leadership.
>
> —LORI GONZALEZ, SUPERINTENDENT

Social Media Best Practices

You don't need to be a full-on influencer out the gate. At the end of the day, pick one platform, create a professional account, get comfortable, and establish a system that works for you. Posting two or three times per week is a great goal when you're starting out. The best advice we can give is to know your audiences for each platform and vary your content to interest them.

Here are some great, easy ideas for posts:

- Motivation Monday: Post great inspirational quotes about leadership and teamwork.
- Thursday Thoughts: An opportunity for short-form videos to connect with your audience.
- Flashback Fridays: Post about your early career days or alumni posts from your site or organization.

You can use scheduling tools to simplify posting, like Buffer, Hootsuite, and Later. These tools make life on social media way easier.

Additionally—Canva for the win! Canva makes content social media sized, which saves so much time.

Make a plan, be consistent, and before you know it, you will be a social butterfly on several platforms.

> Social media has allowed me to build my own network of support that is focused on shared common goals and beliefs. I think hashtags are important. People new to your brand should have a place to curate who you are, and hashtags can tell that story. Keep it short and consistent.
>
> **—DR. NYREE CLARK, COORDINATOR OF EQUITY AND ACCESS**

Lynette

I have been using social media personally since the MySpace days. It was a great way to keep connected with family and friends, and I enjoyed the communities I was a part of. In its infancy, social media may not have had much substance, but it was a whole lot of fun!

Fast-forward to my ten years working at a large urban high school: The principal I was working with saw the need for the school to have a social media presence but didn't have the time or interest to get a page going. Little did I know this would be one of those early moments that helped shape the trajectory my career was going to take many years later. I took the idea and ran with it. I quickly figured out some marketing strategies to make the Facebook page something families would want to be a part of, and I found a way to make the school's Instagram interesting enough that students might find it kind of cool.

These early days of strategizing just based on what seemed to work and creating a hashtag after reading a few articles on the rationale behind them gave me the confidence with social media I would need later. When Superintendent Almendarez challenged me to assist him on a much larger scale, I was able to say yes without reservation. After all, I had already done this for years at the high school! Of course, higher-level social media marketing required me to take some courses, really learn the basics of marketing, and build that car as I was driving it, but I wouldn't change that for anything.

Social media gave me my wings to fly and connect with people in a way nothing else had. I am grateful for my circle, who encouraged me to get on Twitter, which just blew my mind and really opened up my world. Without Twitter I honestly don't think you'd be reading my words right now, since that is how I met THE Dr. Renae Bryant. The rest is history. All of this to say: Social media can be a complete game changer. The platforms are free, and the networks created with them can be deep and meaningful.

You may not be a person who wants to be on all of the platforms, and that's OK. You don't have to do all of the things—but try some of them! Find your niche and make the best profile you can. As Adam Welcome says, "Just start!"

TIPS, STRATEGIES, AND REFLECTIONS

- What platform do you plan to start with? There is no wrong answer when telling your story!

- Make sure the accounts you set up are professional.

   This is not the place to follow your favorite music artists but a place to follow those who will help you professionally.

- As Adam Welcome and Dave Burgess both say, "Just start." Don't wait until the perfect moment. Just open an account.

- You don't have to follow a lot of people at first. Just lurk on social media and get a feel for it.

- Find someone you admire in the education social media sphere and watch what they do. What can you adopt from them? Who do they follow?

- Determine your why, what, and how for each platform. Then post accordingly.

Please share your reflections using the #EdBranding hashtag and visit EdBranding.net for more ideas on social media platforms.

4

THE VALUE
OF A PLN

A professional learning network (PLN) holds significant value for educators and professionals in various fields. A PLN is a personalized network of colleagues, experts, and resources that individuals build and maintain to support their continuous professional development. PLNs often consist of educators from various schools, districts, or institutions. This cross-institutional learning can broaden educators' perspectives and help them understand different educational contexts. Interacting with passionate and dedicated educators in a PLN can inspire and motivate individuals to excel in their profession and make a positive impact on their students' lives.

Social media is probably one of the best and easiest ways to connect with educators from throughout the world to get new ideas, learn that you're not alone, or just see where your district is in the context of other similar districts. With social media, a PLN allows educators to connect with professionals from different backgrounds, experiences, and locations. This diversity of perspectives can enrich discussions, spark new ideas, and expose individuals to a wide range of leadership methods and strategies.

A well-rounded PLN fosters a collaborative environment where educators can share ideas, seek advice, and offer support to one another.

This support system can be invaluable, especially during challenging times in the education profession. PLNs provide access to a wealth of resources such as articles, books, webinars, online courses, and other educational materials. Members of the network can share valuable resources that they discover and find useful.

Overall, a well-nurtured professional learning network can empower educators, enhance their leadership practices, and contribute to their overall professional satisfaction and success. It is important for educators to actively participate in their PLNs, contribute meaningfully, and be open to learning from others.

> In March 2020, I decided to get on Twitter. I wanted to connect with other educators. As I started navigating threads and information, I connected with so many leaders providing innovative ways of support to their sites and districts. I met so many wonderful leaders in person in California. That has been the best part about social media. I now have a support system I can call or message.
>
> **—ROSALBA RODRIGUEZ, PRINCIPAL**

Stealing with Integrity

Lynette

Some of my best marketing ideas have come from the Twitter (X) circles I'm a part of. We recently interviewed Dr. Ray Sanchez, superintendent of the Public Schools of the Tarrytowns, and he put it best when he said that we in education "swipe" from each other. He defined this as stealing ideas but with integrity. This made me laugh

> **"Personal support groups are one of the most powerful ways of gaining wisdom and advice that will help you grow as a leader.**
>
> —BILL GEORGE, AUTHOR, PROFESSOR, CEO **"**

because part of the draw of social media for someone in a creative role such as mine is the ability to see what others are doing, see what works or could work in the districts I serve, and then re-create things to fit our needs. At the most basic level, a PLN is really a great place to go for ideas, collaboration, or even commiseration.

The PLNs I am a part of online have been some of the most motivating and supportive groups of people in my life. I can honestly say my career wouldn't be on the track it is currently on without my PLN. People who get it and are just a DM, text, or email away.

Seeing other people innovate sparks a flame in me to do the same. Find your PLN and truly unleash the creativity within you.

One of my PLN members who I can't live without is Christine Stephens, public information officer for Redlands Unified School District. She and I "swipe" from each other all the time! Here, she discusses the level of preparation that goes into the campaigns you see communications professionals run.

The Redlands Unified School District (RUSD) faced postpandemic challenges, grappling with vacant positions crucial for effective education, specifically school bus drivers and paraprofessionals. To address this issue, a collaborative effort between human resources and the Communications Department led to the creation of the "Day in the Life" campaign. This initiative aimed to bolster hiring endeavors and foster employee retention by showcasing the benefits of working part-time within the district. Targeting potential candidates in the community, the campaign culminated in a job fair.

Initial research pinpointed critical vacancies. Local school district salary research and budget adjustments, overseen by business services, were undertaken to remain competitive within the educational job market.

Thorough planning involved a committee representing various departments, finalizing job fair specifics, and selecting aspects of positions to highlight. The campaign's thematic timeline was crafted, utilizing current employees for marketing purposes and capturing authentic day-in-the-life experiences through videos. Implementation commenced with pre–job fair promotions across social media, press releases to local newspapers, and dissemination of informative flyers. A well-coordinated effort featured banners outside the district office and encouraged official announcements at board meetings.

The campaign's evaluation showcased its triumph. The "Day in the Life" series resulted in hiring five bus drivers and thirty paraprofessionals. Future plans involve extending the concept to highlight other departments such as Child Nutrition Services, Maintenance and Operations as well as clerical positions.

In this endeavor, branding played a pivotal role, elevating the district's image, enhancing recruitment efforts, and effectively communicating the advantages of joining the RUSD team to potential employees within the community.

—CHRISTINE STEPHENS, PUBLIC INFORMATION OFFICER

Professional Learning without Borders

Renae

Dufour's professional learning communities (PLCs) was seminal work to get educators out of their siloes, learning from each other, and collaborating for the benefit of their scholars, colleagues, families, and greater communities. Professional learning networks (PLNs) are an expanded version of this concept. In an organization we can suffer from "that's the way we always have done it." It is important that we are constantly learning from others, reflecting, and calibrating. Where PLCs are based at sites or districts, PLNs have no such boundaries or borders. Your PLN is on social media, made up of folks from professional organizations, advocacy groups, nonprofits, book chats (Leadership Book Chats), Twitter (X) chats, groups around hashtags (like #TLAP, #LeadLAP, #SuptChat, and more)—basically anyone, anywhere you can learn from.

> Social media has allowed me to build trust as a leader, an expert, and a valuable resource to connections in my professional field (association management) as well as to the member community I serve at ACSA. It is a platform where I am able to tell my story, share my core values, and show my own journey and growth. And because it is such a public space, it has allowed others, especially other cabinet-level leaders, to find and connect with me, growing my network in numbers and, therefore, adding value to my personal brand.
>
> —MARGARITA CUIZON-ARMELINO, DEPUTY EXECUTIVE DIRECTOR, ASSOCIATION OF CALIFORNIA SCHOOL ADMINISTRATORS (ACSA)

The phrase "six degrees of separation" exists because it's true. We are all only a few connections away from the people who could help our scholars, colleagues, families, and communities. Try to pause and intentionally create that map. What is it that we need? Who are all the people that we know and who do they know who could help us get there? Map this out just like the funny diagram of the "Six Degrees of Kevin Bacon." You might find you are only six degrees of connection or less away from the person who can make a huge difference for your scholars, staff, families, or organization. Then don't forget the law of reciprocity and help connect someone else.

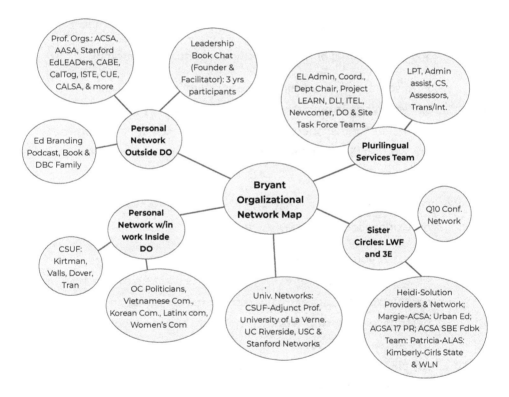

Organizational Network Map Created as an Assignment for the Stanford EdLEADers Organizational Theory Course, 2023.

> In an open culture, the opportunities for learning and relationships are endless. The biggest winners of this sharing revolution are our students. We simply need to embrace what lies at our fingertips.
>
> —GEORGE COUROS, AUTHOR, KEYNOTE SPEAKER, AND PODCASTER

TIPS, STRATEGIES, AND REFLECTIONS

- Create an organizational network or personal network map.

- Join professional organizations (local, state, and national).

- Find someone you admire in the social media education sphere. What organizations or networks are they a part of? Join them. Pay for memberships. The memberships are worth it. You are worth it. Be an active member. Remember to underpromise and over deliver.

- Determine your why, what, and how for each network. Then network accordingly.

- Whether you are in a PLN, a professional organization, or a sister circle, remember to stay "above the line." No matter how comfortable you are with a person, remember this is not a personal relationship. Never complain to anyone. If you need to vent, save it for your mom or significant other. Before you say anything, imagine it as the headline of a newspaper—if you wouldn't want to see that headline, don't say it.

- Give more than you take.

- As you are networking, you are living your brand. Your brand is your reputation.

- No human is perfect. Keep going back to your core values to center and ground yourself.

- As you network, we also recommend reminding yourself daily of Don Miguel Ruiz's four agreements: 1) be impeccable with your word, 2) don't take anything personally, 3) don't make assumptions, and 4) always do your best.[8]

 Please share your reflections using the #EdBranding hashtag and visit EdBranding.net for more ideas on developing your PLN.

---

8   M. Ruiz and N. Wilton, *The Four Agreements: A Practical Guide to Personal Freedom* (San Rafael, CA: Amber-Allen, 2012).

PART II

BRANDING YOUR SITE

"The most important and crucial outcome of a brand presence in education is building powerful community relationships in ways that were not possible before social media. Let the amazing work in your school turn perceptions into reality by developing a well-known brand that your school community can believe in, stand behind and live daily."

—ERIC C. SHENINGER AND THOMAS C. MURRAY IN *LEARNING TRANSFORMED: 8 KEYS TO DESIGNING TOMORROW'S SCHOOLS, TODAY*

5

BRAND YOUR SITE

The Secret Sauce

Lynette

Your site may or may not already have a brand. If it does, I hope it is a positive one. If you need to develop one or reinvent the brand, think of what sets your site apart from others. What is your secret sauce? That is what you lead with!

Every site has hidden gems—those little-known things that make it special. That might be the amazing choir or the academic program that does well but just doesn't advertise all they do. The secret sauce can also be the staff members at your site who just care about their students immensely and have special ways to recognize them throughout the year. I have seen sites whose brand is the STEM school or the performing arts powerhouse in the area. I have also seen sites where the brand is definitely more of a culture thing, like schools that feel like a home away from home. Both types of brands work.

After thinking about what your site's secret sauce is, ask yourself: What do you do better than the schools in your area or even your district? Before you know it, you will have a site brand!

The board of education and superintendent are responsible for the vision of a district, but using social media, you can really emphasize those to the public. You can affect the culture at your site a lot more by displaying your values and beliefs. You will not only show your worth to the BOE but also to your community as a whole. No matter what your site's brand is, be sure to *amplify*! Talk about the things that make your site special and stand out, and talk about them often! Using programs like Class Dojo or Parent Square, you can always be amplifying your brand and what your site stands for. Social media is perfect for this as well, and it's completely free.

Next up is your community—your site is where they are, so connecting with them about it will ensure they feel you are accessible and visible. If it's on Facebook, it's gotta be true, right? So get on Facebook and tell the true story. Many times parents will go to social media first, so why not live in their space?

I am very mindful in my posts to show the diversity of the community of the sites I represent. I am sure to celebrate cultural diversity, showing equity with everything I put out to ensure that when someone sees our feed, they won't have to scroll to a special month or time of year to see themselves represented. The representation is just there, and it's beautiful.

Last but not least is your staff. They are posting and active in these social spaces, so tune in to see what's going on at your sites. Staff members love to receive a virtual pat on the back. Part of leadership is seeing them and what they do and appreciating it. Knowing that makes a world of difference. Use opportunities you see on social media to build relationships and trust. If you see something amazing on social media, take the time to maybe visit that site and tell them about it. Believe me, staff appreciate this a lot. Instead of being seen as the leader who leads from their office, you'll be known as someone who is invested in their success and the success of students as much as they are—an ally instead of "the district."

Rebranding Rebels

Renae

As an organization, Anaheim Union High School District (AUSD) has a set of core values. All communication and branding is filtered through these. When I arrived at Anaheim Union High School, many of the schools were going through a re-visioning process. I was able to be a part of what was happening at Katella High School. This re-visioning was a rebranding. The process was based in Liberatory Design and sought input from those who would be most affected by the changes: staff, scholars, families, and community partners. It was an incredible process to be a part of.

AUHSD Core Values
We believe...

1. In and model the 5 Cs: collaboration, creativity, critical thinking, communication, and compassion

2. That education must work for students and not the other way around.

3. In an assets-based instructional approach focused on our community's strengths and in nurturing everyone's potential

4. In moving the needle toward equity and justice

5. That our vision, mission, and core values are delivered primarily through instruction.

6. In systems not silos

7. Public schools should enhance and strengthen democracy through cultivation of student voice and problem solving

This process looked a little different at Savanna High School. You see, Savanna High School's mascot was the Rebel. Not just any rebel—the mascot painted on the walls and all through Savanna High School was Johnny Rebel. You may or may not know this, but Johnny Rebel is a reference to the Confederacy. Yes, in Anaheim, California, in 2017, there was still a school with Confederate iconography.

Savanna High School is a California State designated Democracy School. So, to AUHSD and Savanna High School's credit, they leaned into the Democracy School practices and put their mascot to a student vote after much research and many presentations. The students voted to keep the "Rebels" name but change the mascot. If we know anything about high schools and alumni, they do not like their mascots changed. There were months of long board of trustees meetings with many public comments. In the end, at a special meeting in a crowded theater at the school, the board voted the same way the students had: to keep the "Rebels" but change the mascot. The controversy and process gained national attention for the positive way the district and site handled the rebranding.

From these mascots painted on the walls of the school:

To this:

You may not have something newsworthy happen at your site, but how are you telling the story of the positive things that *are* happening? As a site leader I was constantly taking photos of scholar and staff events and posting them. The positive news you put out on social media is what Stephen M. R. Covey refers to in *The Speed of Trust* as deposits in your relational account.[9]

When I served as principal at Western High School, I witnessed the awesome tradition that was created before I arrived of honoring a staff member (at the staff meeting) who had used the #LikeAPIO or #WatchWestern hashtags the most. That person would receive a Starbucks gift card. It was a little gamification; and a little gamification is just fine. As a district department leader implementing new programs, I really try to lift the veil on what we do at the district office and give people greater information about the programs we offer and how we serve scholars, families, staff, and community. Teachers and site leaders work tremendously hard. I want to show that at the district level we are working diligently as well.

As a site leader how are you leveraging alumni? There is a tremendous amount of alumni pride for sites and districts. Are you keeping

9   S. M. R. Covey and R. Merrill, *The Speed of Trust: The One Thing That Changes Everything* (New York: Free Press, 2008).

them informed and involved? AUHSD has a very notable list of alumni: David Fletcher, John Stamos, Loretta Sanchez, Gwen Stefani, Eric Stefani, Tiger Woods, Jeff Buckley, Stephen Hillenburg, and countless more. Who are your notable and traditional alumni? How are you connecting with them, communicating with them, and keeping them updated and involved?

What are the vision, mission, and core values of a site? Is your communication and branding aligned?

Branding Inventory

How is your site embracing branding for all the benefits it holds?

1. What is your site's brand?
2. How is your site's brand amplified in the community it serves?
3. Is it current or dated?
4. Who was involved in defining the brand? Should there be more voices involved?
5. Does it meet the RED criteria (relevance, ease, distinctiveness)?

> Marketing and branding is now an essential component of education due to a number of factors, including outside, negative forces and narratives that are not interested in telling all of the positive stories in education.
>
> —JOHN BAUTISTA, AUHSD PUBLIC INFORMATION OFFICER

TIPS, STRATEGIES, AND REFLECTIONS

- What is your site's brand? Does it still represent the scholars, staff, families, and community you serve, or do you need a rebranding?

- Do the staff in your organization at the site level know the brand, the goals, and what they stand for? Can they communicate it clearly?

- If you need to re-vision and rebrand, what process will you use?

- How do you make daily deposits into your relational accounts with scholars, families, staff, and community by sharing the amazing work happening at your site or department?

- Model the way. Get on social media and model the way as a leader using it to own and share the narrative.

- Find those who are willing to help you tell the story and implement a brand ambassador program.

Please share your reflections using the #EdBranding hashtag and visit EdBranding.net for more ideas on branding your site.

6

BUILD YOUR RELATIONSHIPS NOW, NOT WHEN YOU NEED THEM

Establish Trust

Lynette

Building relationships and establishing a strong presence on social media platforms and other communication channels before a crisis occurs will be immensely valuable when you need to navigate difficult situations. When you consistently engage with your audience, share valuable content, and respond to their queries and concerns, you build trust and credibility. This trust can help you during a crisis because people will be more likely to listen to and believe the information you provide. By actively participating in online communities and building relationships with your followers, you can foster a sense of community. When a crisis arises, your community can rally behind you, offer support, and defend your reputation.

During a crisis, timing is crucial. If you already have an established presence on social media platforms, you can quickly disseminate accurate information and updates to your audience, mitigating rumors or false information. This enables you to take control of the narrative and provide timely guidance or reassurance.

Remember, crisis communication is not just about managing a specific crisis—it's an ongoing effort to build and maintain relationships, credibility, and trust with your audience. Regularly engaging with your community, providing valuable content, and demonstrating transparency will strengthen your communication channels and prepare you for any crises that may arise in the future.

Sustaining Relationships

Renae

Build your relationships now, not when you need them—and, I would add, work diligently to maintain them. This applies to your relationships with family, friends, colleagues, networks, community partners, and, of course, the media . . . basically everyone. I still have friendships that began in junior high school and the entertainment industry, and I keep relationships with friends from districts I've previously worked at and with nonprofits I've served.

From my days in music, I knew journalists who covered the entertainment industry. As journalism became consolidated, these same folks began to cover more areas. When I changed careers, these same journalists were willing to allow me to feed stories and photos to them to print, for instance, covering events where students won free student trips to Washington, DC. When I moved to the district level, my best friend from Norco Junior High School, Alicia Lopez, was at the

> # "The most important thing in education is the three Rs: relationships, relationships, relationships.

—DR. ROBERT TAYLOR, SUPERINTENDENT

Los Angeles Times. She helped me get the first article written by Anh Nguyen printed there, which broke the dam open for media coverage for the first Vietnamese DLI program in California. That wouldn't have happened if I hadn't worked on building and sustaining relationships.

Journalists will tell you they are always looking for human interest stories. They love when the public feeds them stories. So don't be shy. If you are in a classroom, calibrate with your principal to find out what the media policy is. If you are a principal, be sure you know the media policy in your district. If you are at a district fortunate enough to have a public information officer, get to know them and their work. Any storytelling you do about your classroom, site, or district is helping them in their role. Build and maintain a relationship with them.

Remember the "no surprise rule" in communication and building and maintaining your relationships. As "flat" as any superintendent says their organization is, there is always a hierarchy to communication: 1) the superintendent (and board), 2) the cabinet, who the superintendent who will communicate with, 3) site and department leaders, who the cabinet will communicate with first before reaching out to union leadership and staff, 4) parents, who will be communicated to after that, 5) then the community and the media.[10] So, ensure that no one along the hierarchy is surprised by what happens.

In Every Crisis Is an Opportunity

In every crisis is an opportunity, a chance to pause, reflect, learn, unlearn, calibrate, and ground ourselves in our core values while leaning into adaptability, openness, flexibility, and strategies like Liberatory Design. What does this have to do with branding self, site, and organization? Everything.

The pandemic was a crisis. It was also a master class in how leaders respond to and leverage crises. Whether they're natural (pandemics,

---

10 Fagen, Friedman, and Fulfrost LLP, Communications (Whittier, CA: ACSA Superintendents Academy Whittier City School District Office, January 20, 2018).

floods, fires, and more) or human generated (shootings, board wars, culture wars, and more), there is no way to avoid crises. With this in mind, the question is, how will we respond to them? You might say that you cannot predict how you will respond to a crisis, but when your brand is centered in your core values and when your work in or around education is scholar centered, then you will know how to respond and you can plan for those responses. In fact, you'll be able to use your value-driven mindset to leverage them.

Renae

It was only a few months after my arrival to the district as a coordinator when I got an urgent call. "The superintendent just received a call from the mayor," he said. "There is a Communist symbol on an example of a Vietnamese marriage license in the *Let's Speak Vietnamese* workbook."

Orange County is the home to the largest Vietnamese population outside of Vietnam. In 1975, Vietnamese refugees fled Vietnam when the Communists took over. Many lost loved ones at the hands of the Communists. Many who fled will never travel back. Many boycott any products produced there. So finding a Communist symbol in a workbook—even one small symbol—was awful.

At the time of the call about the workbook, we had just piloted the second semester of our first Vietnamese world language course. Prior to this we had done our research and vetted the book—the hardcover book. The publisher hadn't given us the workbook. We'd shared the hardcover book with the Dual Language Immersion Task Force. We were all happy with it. Until that call.

"What do we do?" he asked.

We were fortunate it had happened on a Friday before a holiday.

"Pull all the books," I replied. "It was a pilot. We'll pull the books and put together a book-vetting committee for the course and for next

"

More recently as I think about the role of communications, I think increasingly you need to go where the people are . . . I think it's become more dangerous to not go back and post and interact (on social media).

—DR. DON AUSTIN

"

year's program. I will do more research. We'll get samples of different books and have the community decide. They know best."

The books were pulled. The superintendent appeared on the local news and confidently spoke about the situation and putting together a committee to help the district vet and select books that all would deem appropriate.

The next weeks consisted of collecting books from different publishers all over the globe, including Vietnam. Although we knew books from Communist Vietnam wouldn't be approved, we wanted to allow them in the process so the public could vote on what to adopt. My superintendent generously mentored me through the process. Our work included the mayor, his wife, business owners, elders from the Vietnamese language and culture schools, Vietnamese world language teachers from the district our scholars would attend next, our Vietnamese interpreters and translators, teachers with Vietnamese bilingual authorizations, university professors, and more. Thanks to my superintendent's coaching, I was able to run a very smooth book-vetting process, which brought the community together in a spirit of Liberatory Design. Everyone was very happy with the voting results and book decisions. The public information officer pulled me to the side later and told me, "I want to let you know that the mayor, his wife, and Ms. Nguyen spoke very highly of you and the book-vetting process. Good job."

Even better, everyone involved was happy to be asked to share their expertise and to be a part of the process. What started as a newsworthy crisis, where the district was asked if we supported communism, became an opportunity to bring the community together.

Of course, we posted all over social media about the successful book-vetting meeting, adoption process, and selected texts. Opportunity from crisis. What was a moment of crisis was leveraged for greater community partnership, participation, and trust.

TIPS, STRATEGIES, AND REFLECTIONS

- Are you consistently communicating the positive stories from within your organization?

- Is there a two-way communication set up between the organization and the community?

- How are you maintaining the relationships you have built? Do you calendar phone calls or emails to check in on the people in your network?

- How are you proactively building and maintaining your relationships?

Please share your reflections using the #EdBranding hashtag and visit EdBranding.net for more ideas on proactively building and maintaining your relationships.

7

BECOME THE MEDIA

MEDIA TAKEOVER

DIY EDU

Renae

I am old enough that I used to buy fanzines. Fanzines, aka zines, were the blogs, podcasts, and websites of the mid-1990s. You would buy them from concerts or record stores (places you would buy music before iTunes existed—think Rhino Records in Claremont or Amoeba in LA). They are an art form. Some people still make them, and there are still zine fests today (Anaheim Public Library hosted one in August 2023).

The 1990s was a time when alternative culture was growing. Hip-hop and punk rock were becoming mainstream. People were starting their own independent record labels in college dorms, garages, and apartments and putting out music without major corporate approval or financial support. The same thing happened all over the media. There was a message to "do it yourself" (DIY). People didn't need to wait for the blessing of media corporations to publish—they would just start their own magazine. The call was to "become the media" and not allow major media to control the messaging.

We have long since become the media. We can easily start a website, podcast, blog, vlog, social media site, and more. The veil has been permanently pierced and altogether removed. Anyone can be a content creator, and now major media outlets are struggling to stay relevant as they compete with so many niche content creators. Scholars, staff, families, and community members have all become the media. How do we, as public school educators and leaders, leverage this for the benefit of these same scholars, staff, caregivers/families, and community members?

Don't fear the media. Become the media. Empower your scholars and community members to do the same.

At AUHSD, we empower scholars to blog, vlog, and create AUHSD Talks, podcasts, films, and more. Our families are empowered and regularly tell positive stories about district events on their social media in English and Spanish. We are piloting podcasting in our English language development (ELD) courses so our scholars can have greater engagement with a meaningful activity for an authentic audience. We focus on the 5 Cs of communication, creativity, collaboration, critical thinking, and compassion/character/civic engagement. Podcasting offers the 5 Cs in one project-based-learning activity that can make use of Universal Design for Learning (UDL) with project management, script writing, rehearsing, editing, speaking, interviewing, and more. The next step is to empower our families in the same way.

How are you empowering your biggest allies—your scholars, staff, families/caregivers, and community partners—to become the media?

"And if the impression is given that there's some leader or spokesman or something like that organizing, galvanizing things, that's absolutely the wrong lesson. The lesson there is to follow your leader. The lesson ought to be: take your life into your own hands.

—NOAM CHOMSKY

Ideas for Empowering Yourself and Others to Become the Media

- Start a site, school, or district social media ambassador program. Gamify the program to create some fun and friendly competition.
- Offer social media, blogging, vlogging, and podcasting capacity-building for scholars, staff, families/caregivers, and community partners.
- Write a press release to send in to a local paper highlighting something positive about your site (check your district media policy and process before submitting).
- Submit an opinion piece or editorial to your local paper or educational magazine (check your district media policy and process before submitting).

Tell Your Own Story

Lynette

I truly believe that there are major benefits in districts transforming into their own media outlets. This approach allows districts to take charge of their story, highlight achievements and innovations, and find the unique stories that might otherwise go unnoticed in the mainstream media landscape. By becoming the media, districts can directly reach their communities and the broader public without the intermediary of external news sources. This direct line of communication fosters transparency, builds trust, and enhances community engagement. It also allows for a real portrayal of the educational journey, showcasing the complexities and triumphs of the learning process that can often be oversimplified or overlooked by traditional media. Additionally, in an era where misinformation can spread rapidly, having control over their own media channels enables educators to provide accurate, timely information, playing a crucial role in shaping public perception and reinforcing their credibility.

My own experience has shown that an innovative strategy of gamifying social media through competitions can definitely benefit a district. A simple social media competition between school sites created quite the frenzy. Aside from some cool prizes they could win, the bragging rights were all the staff could talk about. I recall the texts and emails I'd receive in anticipation of my announcement for who won each month! Gamification injected an element of fun and engagement into social media that just created better and better content. This strategy not only had the sites creating incredible content regularly, it drove participation and interest among students, parents, and the rest of the community. These competitions generated a buzz around each school site that definitely increased visibility and fostered a sense of pride and belonging within the district.

At a district I started a podcast at, we had students become interested in podcasting! That was a cool by-product of the district having a podcast. Luckily, we had a very awesome chief technology officer, Jamal Boyce. He decided to invest in these students, so any school that was interested in having a podcast received a mobile setup of podcasting equipment and a crash course in how to podcast from myself, him, or our cohost, Dr. Nyree Clark. Talk about truly amplifying student voice. The domino effect of storytelling in that district is strong. From staff to students, that story is being TOLD and really well because it's being told collaboratively.

TIPS, STRATEGIES, AND REFLECTIONS

- Just start. You don't need fancy equipment. You just need Google Meet or Zoom to record a podcast.

- Get organized with a format for scheduling and communicating with podcast guests and writing questions.

- Decide if you will have a video format as well as an audio format and plan your YouTube channel.

- Choose your editing and hosting platform.

- Be consistent! The key to a successful podcast is dropping new content regularly.

- What steps will you take to start your own podcast or to empower others to start one?

 Please share your reflections using the #EdBranding hashtag and visit EdBranding.net for more ideas on starting a podcast or empowering others to do so.

PART III

BRANDING YOUR ORGANIZATION

"Do you work for education or does education work for you?"

—SUPERINTENDENT MICHAEL MATSUDA'S
QUESTION TO THE TWENTY-EIGHT
THOUSAND SCHOLARS AUHSD SERVES

8

BRAND YOUR ORGANIZATION

Branding Is a Must

Renae

Districts often have budgets based, at least in part, on enrollment. In California we are suffering from declining birth rates and declining enrollment, especially in Orange County. Anaheim Union High School District has lost approximately 4,900 scholars since 2011–2012. Future AUHSD enrollment is projected to decline by another 3,900 students through 2026–2027. In the course of fifteen years, AUHSD will have lost approximately 8,900 scholars.

Branding helps districts compete for enrollment. Therefore, it is not a "nice to have" kind of a thing. Branding is a must.

And all of us can do our part in branding our districts. If we do, the brand will expand.

Support, Amplify, Celebrate

Lynette

Branding your organization is interesting because most organizations have an established brand, so you are not necessarily creating branding from the ground up. However, you should be supporting that brand and amplifying it from whatever seat you are leading from. So what follows isn't necessarily a how-to on branding a district but a how-to on how to support the existing brand and how to amplify it well.

One great way to amplify your brand is ensuring that staff and students are aware of it. If there are goals, make them part of staff meetings so that they're universally known. The brand and goals for the organization should not come as a surprise. The more the staff know, the more they can help amplify those goals! And although I am a fan of a good sports rivalry, I do think showcasing what we offer and achieve in the district as a whole is the way to amplify what's going on daily and build positive equity. The social media posts I create for districts are intended to show a team, not pit individual schools against each other.

I have worked with several organizations throughout California on amplifying their already existing brands. This is where alignment matters! If your organization is already well established, keep the branding—just support it in all you do. If there are particular goals, mission statements, or promises made to the organization's clients, then those items should be reflected in each meeting you hold as well as in any social media. For example, if you are an organization who has goals for student success and wellness, your posts should be explicit in how they align to those goals or values. This way the mission statement or board goals and priorities are not just something discussed at the kick-off meeting and never again. Put them at the forefront, where people are seeing them talked about all year and seeing real, tangible examples of them in all you do.

One of the best ways I've found to support an organization's brand is to implement the kind of brand ambassador program I discussed earlier, in the sites section. When I did that, I decided to create a handbook describing the program and I really talked up the skills the volunteers would learn, the network we'd create, and the abundance of stories we'd get to tell together. Once I did all of this, I got started developing what the professional development portion would look like. It was fun to create the courses, which included a core four: an intro to social media marketing for schools, Facebook, Instagram, and Twitter. I polled the group to see what they wanted to learn, and I'd create professional development around whatever topic won each month. I cannot even begin to share the benefits of this program, from building capacity to creating a PLN within your own district and of course the rich stories being shared on all social media platforms. As Renae has pointed out to me, the true test of my leadership and innovation is that these programs continue to be successful even after I've left the district. The relationships built within the program and the wonderful array of stories told by real staff throughout the district is just beautiful.

I can tell a great story on my own, but the story we tell together is more powerful and diverse than what any one person can tell. Of course, diversity isn't only important in telling the story; showcasing the diversity that exists within your district is important, too. Highlight it! Celebrate it often and loudly. Everyone loves looking at feeds that are authentically diverse, where you can see and feel the culture that exists in a place and see yourself reflected in what is celebrated in a district.

So while you don't need to brand most existing organizations, your work can fully support the brand that already exists.

Rebranding

Renae

When I was recruited to AUHSD, the district had so many incredible things happening, but you would not know it from the website and social media.

That changed at a professional learning event I attended at the Anaheim Convention Center. One of the keynote speakers was Ryan Holiday, who at that point had been director of marketing for American Apparel and an apprentice to Robert Greene, the author of *The 48 Laws of Power*. Ryan Holiday is the author of *Trust Me, I'm Lying: Confessions of a Media Manipulator*, *Growth Hacker Marketing*, and *Ego Is the Enemy*, among many other excellent books, and he hosts the *Daily Stoic* podcast. We were all very inspired by his keynote, but we were also left wondering where to start. That's when one of our teacher leaders approached us and offered to set up a meeting for AUHSD with her husband, Ken Muench, CEO of advertising firm Collider (and coauthor of *R.E.D. Marketing: The Three Ingredients of Leading Brands*).

Collider ended up taking AUHSD under their wing. The district went from having several logos, which had been developed over decades, to one new logo. Collider also helped AUHSD create a new motto that focused on the significance and purpose of the district: "Unlimited You." This led to a rebranding campaign across the district. Now, thanks to the excellent work of John Bautista, AUHSD's public information officer, and his team—Dulce Torre, Ronnie Galang, and Mary Pearson—AUHSD has a complete communications plan, which includes social media strategies, a brand style guide, a crisis communications plan, and a site/district directory.

From these AUHSD logos:

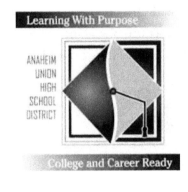

To these AUHSD logos:

The pandemic and social unrest of 2020 inspired another round of rebranding for AUHSD. This time it was about mission and vision. We would also add core values. We went from the vision/mission every district had of making students "college and career ready" to something that truly reflected the 2021 version of AUHSD.

AUHSD MISSION
The Anaheim Union High School District, in partnership with the greater community, will graduate socially aware, civic-minded students who are life ready by cultivating the soft and hard skills.

AUHSD VISION

To create a better world through Unlimited You

AUHSD Core Values
We believe...

1. In and model the 5 Cs: collaboration, creativity, critical thinking, communication, and compassion

2. That education must work for students and not the other way around.

3. In an assets-based instructional approach focused on our community's strengths and in nurturing everyone's potential

4. In moving the needle toward equity and justice

5. That our vision, mission, and core values are delivered primarily through instruction.

6. In systems not silos

7. Public schools should enhance and strengthen democracy through cultivation of student voice and problem solving

Example of Organization Branding Communications
(Bryant, Jackson, Mayfield, and Root, 2019)

Audience	Purpose	Format/Types of Messages	Frequency
Board of Education	Strengthen Governance Team access to accurate and succinct information thereby maintaining shared knowledge of issues, initiatives, and recognitions relevant to the district and school communities	Response and updates to Board Members' questions/inquiries Board awareness of issues occurring in the school and school community State and local recognitions District/school events, programs, and celebrations Dates/invitation to events sponsored by the City, community and local elected official Updates on the District Strategic Plan/LCAP	Weekly
Superintendent's Cabinet and District Leaders	Ensure a common message to all contingents by providing information for the superintendent to report to the Board, staff and community	Assistant Superintendents and department leaders provide updates related to district programs, accountability data, responses to Board questions, etc. Information is disseminated to the Board and school community (principals, employees, parents, and community), if appropriate Social media is used as vital communication outlet Banners and signage are used to convey the Single Story at District, City and Community Events	Weekly

Principals	A formal structure to ensure administrators are knowledgeable of district events and celebrations	Celebrations of successes Recognitions Innovative practices	Weekly
Bargaining Units/ Employees	Convey consistent information to all employees about the district story and initiatives	Celebrations of successes Recognitions Innovative practices	Weekly
Parents, Guardians and Community Members	Share the district story	Digital Media: District and school websites, Electronic Newsletter, Peachjar Fliers (or similar platforms) Email: Email lists Print Media: Newsletters, brochures, fliers, posters Social Media: Facebook, Twitter, Instagram, YouTube Phone Apps: Blackboard Connect, Remind Meetings: Board Meetings, Committee Meetings, Parent Workshops, Community Forums News media: Press release, local cable stations	Ongoing

Community (e.g., elected officials, realtors, businesses, etc.)	Superintendent communicates the Single Story to a broader community	Magazine/brochure is mailed and/or sent electronically to parents, community members residing within the district's zip code, city officials, local business, and service clubs/ organizations, include pictures and announcements of award-winning schools and district programs	Quarterly

AI and Branding

Lynette

In the rapidly evolving digital landscape, AI has emerged as a transformative tool for branding and marketing, particularly on social media platforms. AI's ability to analyze large volumes of data and generate insights can be harnessed to create more personalized, targeted, and effective branding strategies. For instance, AI algorithms can sift through social media data to understand consumer behaviors, preferences, and trends, enabling brands to tailor their messaging and content to resonate more deeply with their audience. This data-driven approach not only enhances the relevance of marketing efforts but also ensures that the brand stays agile and responsive to changing consumer sentiments and market dynamics.

For the work I do, AI plays a crucial role in optimizing the content and timing of social media posts. With its ability to analyze engagement patterns and predict peak activity times, AI can help me schedule posts for maximum visibility and interaction, a key factor in building a strong social media presence. I really use AI to analyze things I've already written, but sometimes it's a great thought partner if I'm stuck on a caption. AI is a wonderful tool to help you stay consistent with your branding in your messaging as an organization. One rule of thumb for using an AI is edit, edit, and EDIT. Do not copy and paste. Other than that, have fun, keep an open mind, and let it help you!

Renae

AUHSD is always innovating. In 2021, AUHSD was the first district to form a partnership with Google to offer Google Certificates in high school. Before the pandemic, AUHSD partnered with eKadence to launch a nonprofit learning management system based on teacher leader input. AUHSD was early to create an artificial intelligence (AI) pathway, starting one in 2021, and we had an AI conference the next academic year. Some were not excited and actually questioned the money spent on this.

All that changed in December 2022 when everyone started talking about ChatGPT. To be honest, the first time I heard of ChatGPT was from our chief technology officer Erik Greenwood in December 2022 at our weekly education division meeting. Everyone listened to him, but no conversation happened. We just went on to the next topic. The next time I heard about it was days later while listening to the *School PR* podcast. I understood at that moment why Erik was interested in it and the impact it would have on scholars, staff, families, and the community.

Matt Miller, in his book *AI for Educators: Learning Strategies, Teacher Efficiencies, and a Vision for an Artificial Intelligence Future,* lays out thirty ways AI can support teaching and learning. Here are some ways he suggests AI can be used that support educational branding:

- Use AI as a deeper source of information than Google.
- Use AI for lots of good examples.
- Use AI to remix your work.

- Use AI to write letters of recommendation.[11]

And here are some more:

- Use AI to write press releases.
- Use AI to write crisis communications.
- Use AI to write social media posts.
- Use AI to create presentation slides.
- Use AI to write grant applications.
- Use AI to write award nominations.
- Use AI to write articles.
- Use AI to write letters to the community.
- Use AI as a brainstorming partner.

Of course, after using any of these strategies with AI, it's important to go back and add your own voice to the product.

In the 2023 book *AI Classroom: The Ultimate Guide to Artificial Intelligence in the Classroom*, Amanda Fox poses questions every educator should ask about AI:

1. Can AI create this for me?
2. Can I work with AI to do this?

She also poses questions for teachers regarding scholars and AI. I've adapted these and changed Fox's verbiage from "students" to "I."

1. How will I use AI to learn?
2. How will I develop skills to help me leverage AI?
3. Have I considered the ethics of the AI I am using?
4. Are there any up-to-date AI tools I should know about?
5. Am I involving scholars, staff, families, and community members in the design and evaluation of AI tools?
6. Am I using AI in a way that promotes collaboration, critical thinking, and problem solving?

---

11 M. Miller, *AI for Educators: Learning Strategies, Teacher Efficiencies, and a Vision for an Artificial Intelligence Future* (San Diego, CA: Ditch That Textbook, 2023).

7. Am I using design thinking and specifically Liberatory Design when using AI tools?[12]

At the virtual CUE AI Conference, Joe Marquez emphasized the key to using generative AI is to get good at prompting. He offered that there is a "cadence to prompt engineering."

1. Task: Use an action verb and describe what you want it to do.
2. Context: Give very specific context, like time period, state, grade level, audience.
3. Exemplar: Add an example, rubric, standards, framework, etc.
4. Persona: Write in a particular voice (e.g., someone like Delores Huerta).
5. Format: Specify a length and form (e.g., a one-paragraph summary).
6. Tone: Indicate the kind of output you'd like (e.g., creative writing, evaluation, etc.).

I was not born with technology in my hands, so like many others I always have a learning curve. Our advice is to get in the sandbox and play. You won't break it, and your scholars are already using it.

Branding Inventory

How is your organization embracing branding for all the benefits it holds?

1. What is your organization's brand?
2. How is your organization's brand amplified in the community it serves?
3. Is it current or dated?
4. Who was involved in defining the brand? Should there be more voices involved?

---

12 D. Fitzpatrick, A. Fox, and B. Weinstein, *The AI Classroom: The Ultimate Guide to Artificial Intelligence in Education* (Beechgrove, IN: TeacherGoals Publishing, 2023).

5. Does it meet the RED criteria (relevance, ease, distinctiveness)?
6. How are you leveraging AI to assist you with branding?

 Please share your reflections using the #EdBranding hashtag and visit EdBranding.net for more ideas on branding your organization.

9

LIBERATORY DESIGN, STREET DATA, COMMUNITY SCHOOLS, AND BRANDING

Does Education Work for You or with You?

Renae

What do Liberatory Design, street data, and community schools have to do with educational branding? I would say everything.

I first learned about Liberatory Design (mindsets and modes to design for equity) from Dr. Olympia Kyriakidis during the pandemic. AUHSD Plurilingual Services was a part of the Multilingual California Project (MCaP) Grant via Orange County Department of Education and the California Association of Bilingual Educators (CABE). At one of the first virtual convenings, we were fortunate to have our capacity built by the incredible Dr. Kyriakidis, executive director of equity, multilingual education, and global achievement with San Diego County Office of Education.

Dr. Kyriakidis has a special place in my heart. In 2014 she was the principal at Riverview International Academy in Lakeside Union School District, the first site we visited before we implemented Vietnamese DLI at WSD. Visiting her site, which was all DLI (parents chose Spanish DLI or Mandarin DLI), made us know what we were doing was possible. We spent a day at her site visiting classrooms and then debriefing with her. That day was a master class in DLI implementation, program sustainability, and growth. When she began leading the site, they were in declining enrollment. After implementing Spanish DLI and then Mandarin DLI, it was so successful they grew from 900 students to 1,200 students, had to have two campuses (one for K–1 and another for 2–6), and had no English-only track.

Needless to say, I love this woman and I was eager to learn from her. She introduced Liberatory Design, telling us it was founded at the National Equity Project and based on the design thinking work out of the Stanford Design School. Liberatory Design is the result of a collaboration between Tania Anaissie, David Clifford, Susie Wise, and the National Equity Project (Victor Cary and Tom Malarkey).

So, what is Liberatory Design and what does it have to do with educational branding? Liberatory Design is a process and practice to:

- Generate self-awareness to liberate designers from habits that perpetuate inequity
- Shift the relationship between the people who hold power to design and those impacted
- Foster learning and agency for those involved in and influenced by the design work
- Create conditions for collective liberation

When we think of educational branding, we must think of it through the lens of Liberatory Design. Many of us do not live in the communities that we serve. It is extremely important that we come to our work with Liberatory Design mindsets. Liberatory Design mindsets express the spirit of the process of Liberatory Design:

- Build relational trust
- Practice self-awareness
- Recognize oppression
- Embrace complexity
- Focus on human values
- Seek liberatory collaboration
- Work with fear and discomfort
- Attend to healing
- Work to transform power
- Exercise creative courage
- Take action to learn
- Share, don't sell

As we tell the story of the site, department, or district, how are we not only centering the voices of those most affected but also empowering them to tell their stories? How do we seek input from those most impacted?

We can do this through Liberatory Design modes:

- Notice by practicing self-awareness, seeking the context about the systems you design within, and exploring the history of oppression in those systems to develop an equity-based identity.
- Reflect on team health, design intention, and the impact our design process is having on us individually, interpersonally, institutionally, and systemically to support continual growth and healing.

- See the system, enabling us to identify potential equity challenges, what about the system is protruding these, and what we need to learn more about as we engage in empathy work.
- Empathize from a place of love, respect, and curiosity. Design opportunities to understand the experiences, emotions, and motivations of the person or community you are designing with.
- Define and develop a point of view about the assets, challenges, and needs with the community. Together, look for patterns and insights in stories that reveal the deeper needs of the people closest to the challenge.
- Inquire when the way ahead is not clear. Inquire to help you better understand and define the challenge to provide a clearer direction for your prototyping.
- Imagine by creating time to brainstorm and imagine "what if?" This can unlock and unleash the creative courage that will lead to innovative approaches and solutions to equity challenges.
- Prototype by building rough versions of what you're working on to test key ideas. Designing for equity requires creative experimentation.
- Try by gathering feedback about prototypes to check your assumptions and intentions. Feedback is a gift used to improve whatever is being designed and ensure that the design is attuned to stated equity goals.[13]

Liberatory Design is key to educational branding. Many people who work in a district don't always live in that same district. Even if we do, our experiences as school staff are different from those of our scholars and caregivers. As we tell the story of the site, department, or district how are we intentionally using Liberatory Design and designing *with* people and not *for* them? How are we coming to the work with

---

13 T. Anaissie, V. Cary, D. Clifford, T. Malarkey, and S. Wise, *Liberatory Design*, 2021, http://www.liberatorydesign.com.

a Liberatory Design mindset? How are we empowering these groups with agency to tell their own stories whenever possible?

You can download the free Liberatory Design deck at liberatorydesign.com. The deck is under the Creative Commons license. Use, share, and give credit. Use alone or use with scholars, staff, families and/or community.

Street Data

Renae

What is street data and what does it have to do with educational branding?

During the pandemic in 2021, the incomparable authors Shane Safir and Jamila Dugan published *Street Data: A Next-Generation Model for Equity, Pedagogy, and School Transformation.* The authors describe three different types of data: satellite, map, and street. Satellite data give us lagging indicators—think yearly mandated standardized assessments, attendance patterns, graduation rates, teacher retention, principal attrition, and caregiver participation rates. Map data is "closer to the ground." It gives information about trends within a learning community: running records, formative assessments, exit tickets, common assessments, and survey data around scholar, caregiver, and/or staff perceptions. Street data, as described by Safir and Dugan, is the qualitative data found in: 1) audio interviews of scholars, staff, or parents (think empathy interviews and oral histories), 2) listening campaigns or focus groups, 3) equity participation trackers, 4) ethnographies—deep exploration of scholar groups on campus, 5) "fishbowls" to draw out experiences and perspectives, 6) home visits, 7) shadowing students or staff, 8) equity-focused classroom scans, 9) structured observations of meetings, and 10) scholar-led community walks.[14]

At AUHSD we are diligently working to make street data a priority. Our community schools coordinators and community schools teacher leads held empathy interviews using Liberatory Design to codesign what they thought community schools should offer as well as what they considered to be the assets in the community. Superintendent Matsuda holds listening campaigns with affinity groups of caregivers to know what their unique input and concerns are.

Diana Fujimoto (AUHSD's professional learning coordinator) and I were trained by Dr. Ivannia Soto (who wrote the books *ELL Shadowing as a Catalyst for Change* and *Shadowing Multilingual Learners*). We facilitate plurilingual (English learner) shadowing professional learning with our 5 Cs coaches. They then facilitate the same professional learning with their staff, who then do shadowing of an experienced plurilingual professional to truly empathize with the scholar experience and create a sense of urgency for more scholar speaking time.

For an equity participation tracker, we have partnered with TeachFX, whose app allows staff to record their classes or meetings and gives them a report on how much they have spoken compared to the scholars. The app also provides a recording of the conversation so staff can reflect on the quality of the conversations as well. The district sees aggregate user data but never sees the data of an individual staff member. Each AUHSD site has facilitated community schools bus tours led by their community schools coordinator, principal, and a scholar, focusing on the assets of that specific community.

The purpose of street data is to uplift the voices of scholars, caregivers, staff, and community. This is the purpose of educational branding leadership as well. How are we lifting the voices of scholars, caregivers, staff, and community as we share the positive narratives of our sites, departments, or districts? How are we empowering these same people

---

14 S. Safir and J. Dugan, *Street Data: A Next Generation Model for Equity, Pedagogy, and School Transformation* (Thousand Oaks, CA: Corwin, 2021).

with agency to tell their stories? How are we collaborating with them to codesign these efforts? How do we seek their input on the assets they see in their communities?

Community Schools

Renae

What are community schools and what do they have to do with educational branding?

Community schools have existed for years and are based on four guiding pillars: integrated services, including trauma-informed health services; expanded learning time and opportunities; collaborative leadership and practices for educators and administrators to support school climate; and engaging students, families, and the community. Through the California Community Schools Partnership Program (CCSPP) grant, AUHSD received $25 million to fund thirteen community schools.

Branding (aligning values, vision, mission, and narratives) was extremely important in this process. Gathering scholars, staff, caregivers/families, and community partners, a Community Schools Task Force was formed. In this process, each member became an ambassador to communicate the initial vision, mission, values, and objectives of AUHSD community schools. Branding was used to center Liberatory Design and uplift community voice through map-data methods and street data methods. As AUHSD was branding to the scholars, caregivers/families, staff, and community, the district was also helping to refine the brand and narrative to center it in their voice. AUHSD was also branding to the larger educational community, inviting districts to join our community schools tours (and of course building the plane as we flew it, like all districts do). The objective is to have AUHSD centered as a learning lab (think the UCLA Teaching and Learning Lab) and monetize our services. We host so many districts. I host at least ten districts a year to show secondary dual language immersion. We've branded like a business with flyers for the visits with all the information.

Liberatory Design, street data, and community schools are approaches we need to take to make educational branding authentically centered on the scholars, caregivers/families, staff, and community that we serve.

AUHSD Community Schools leading the way

- Opportunity for Community School Sites

- Internal Leading/Learning Lab: Thursday, 8/31/23 (8am - 12pm)

- First w/Outside guests: 9/21/23 (Magnolia HS)

Branding as a Tool for Commitment

Lynette

Equity in education is not just about providing equal access to resources; it's about acknowledging and addressing the unique needs, strengths, and cultural backgrounds of each student. Liberatory Design, a concept central to this chapter, advocates for a rethinking of educational systems to make them more inclusive and responsive to the needs of diverse communities. It's about creating spaces that empower all students, especially those from marginalized groups, to become active agents in their learning process. Meanwhile, street data refers to the qualitative, ground-level insights gathered from students, parents, and teachers, offering a more nuanced and humancentric view of educational success beyond traditional metrics.

Branding in this context transcends the conventional idea of marketing. It's about how schools and educational institutions are perceived in terms of their commitment to equity and inclusivity. A brand built on the principles of Liberatory Design and informed by street data is inherently community focused. It resonates with the values, aspirations, and lived experiences of the community it serves. Community schools, which are deeply embedded in their local contexts and actively involve community members in their operations, epitomize this approach. They become more than places of learning; they are vibrant hubs where the lines between education, social justice, and community engagement blur. Such schools, through their branding, communicate a powerful message: that education is a collaborative, community-driven endeavor that values and uplifts every individual, thereby contributing to a more equitable society.

We'd love for the leaders reading this to reenvision branding not just as a tool for public image but as a reflection of their deep commitment to creating equitable, inclusive, and community-empowered educational spaces. I consider these practices with each of my social media posts. I try to showcase the equitable practices within our community as well as ensuring that we value all voices and that everyone can see themselves reflected in the stories I tell. This is something that is incredibly important to me and also something that I firmly believe creates a story everyone is a part of.

TIPS, STRATEGIES, AND REFLECTIONS

- Facilitate empathy interviews or other street data collection methods to better understand the assets and objectives of your scholars, staff, caregivers/families, and community members.

- Start a brand ambassador program with scholars, staff, caregivers, and community members. Provide ongoing, consistent, high-quality professional learning for them.

- Empower scholars, caregivers, and staff to start their own podcasts.

- Encourage and empower scholars, caregivers, and staff to write blogs, editorials, opinion pieces, and articles.

 Please share your reflections using the #EdBranding hashtag and visit EdBranding.net for more ideas on integrating Liberatory Design, street data, and the community schools approach into your educational branding.

10

BOND, SCHOOL BOND

Proactive Bonding

Renae

I remember driving to my mom's house calling Lynette, giddily. "We have to include a chapter about how important education branding is to passing school bonds, and I have the perfect name for it: 'Bond, School Bond.'"

In California, school districts desperately need school bonds to pass to fund facilities projects, modernization, and more. Just like you need to build relationships now, not when you need them, you cannot wait until you need to pass a bond to start communicating to the community all of the great things the district does for the scholars, staff, caregivers/families, and community. You have to consistently communicate the story of all the value added by the district to the community. The community includes caregivers/parents, as well as residents who are childless, retired, or with non–school-age children. How are we proactively communicating and building relationships with these

residents and doubling down our efforts on those you know will support a bond if communicated to and given information?

What's a Bond?

According to the EdSource glossary, a school bond is, "A method
of borrowing employed by school districts to pay for a large capital
investment, used in much the same way as a person who takes out a
mortgage to purchase a home."[15] Since 2001, voters in a school district
can authorize a local general obligation bond with a 55 percent super-
majority vote. In the past, a two-thirds vote was required. Districts can
choose to seek bond passage with either a two-thirds vote or a 55 percent vote that requires greater accountability measures. The principal
and interest are repaid by local property owners through an increase
in property taxes. A simple majority of state voters must approve a
state general obligation bond, which is repaid by state taxes and has no
impact on property tax rates.

You cannot write a book about educational branding without
including a chapter about how it is related to school bonds and/
or taxpayers' money overall. In California specifically, school bonds
are the way we are able to improve our facilities. Though elections
can be volatile, unpredictable, complex, and ambiguous (VUCA),
bonds must communicate vision, understanding, clarity, and agility
(VUCA flipped).

How to Brand a Bond

Renae

The first time I heard of a school bond was while I was still
a teacher and a Corona-Norco Teachers Association site

---

15 https://edsource.org/glossary

representative. I was asked to phonebank and encourage my colleagues to do the same. I remember calling residents for hours. We were fortunate that the community supported the measure and many schools received the improvements they needed. The next time a bond came up, I was a site leader. It was when I was a leader at the district level that there was a pulling-back-the-curtain moment about bonds. So many times educators say, "You don't know, what you don't know." This was one of those times.

When I became a director, we worked on the Measure T Bond in Westminster School District. It passed in favor of issuing $76 million in bonds to upgrade schools, provide heat and air conditioning, and improve student access to technology. A lot of work off school property and beyond school hours was done—all volunteer work. Many relationships were leveraged as well. The district told its story of added value consistently before, during, and after bond measures were on the ballot. The community understood, because all of the programs, supports, and upgrades the district wanted to do were on the website, social media, and newsletters, and were featured on mainstream media as well as in smaller outlets. Once the bond passed, the district supported cameras live streaming the construction, so anyone at any time could go online and see where their tax dollars were going.

Palo Alto USD provides weekly updates with current photos on their construction projects on their websites. Another district explicitly connects the funding to projects with videos of scholars and staff in action that explain the funding and then explain the project and how the funding is supporting scholars, staff, and the greater learning community. You can provide detailed information about upcoming projects, broken out by school, on your website and update it often. You can create branded PDFs for each school site and explain the particular projects for specific schools, as well as those they feed into and allow families to easily determine exactly how the bond will impact their own children over time.[16]

Bonding with AI

Renae

To demonstrate that I am practicing what I preached in the section on AI, here are the tips ChatGPT gave me when I gave it the following prompt: "best branding strategies to pass a school bond in California."[17]

Passing a school bond in California, or anywhere else, requires a well-thought-out branding and communication strategy to gain community support. Here are some effective strategies:

Community Engagement and Needs Assessment

Begin by conducting surveys and holding community meetings to understand the specific needs of your school district. This will help you tailor your bond proposal to address these needs and demonstrate your commitment to the community.[18]

---

16 M. Hite, "What to Do After Your School Bond Election—However It Went," SchoolCEO, 2023, www.schoolceo.com/a/what-to-do-after-your-schoo l-bond-election-however-it-went.

17 Since there is no way to cite ChatGPT, I have provided citations to where these ideas originated.

18 K12 Insight, *School Bond Campaigns,* 2018, https://www.k12insight.com/news/ school-bond-campaigns/.

Create a Strong Brand Identity

Develop a compelling brand identity for your campaign. This includes a memorable logo, slogan, and campaign materials that visually and emotionally resonate with your audience.[19]

Educational Campaign

Inform the community about the importance of the bond and how it will benefit students, teachers, and the community as a whole. Use a mix of presentations, flyers, brochures, and digital channels to communicate your message.[20]

Website and Social Media

Create a dedicated website and social media profiles for your campaign. Use these platforms to provide updates, share success stories, and engage with the community. Leverage social media advertising to target specific demographics.[21]

Coalition Building

Build a coalition of supporters, including parents, teachers, local business owners, and community leaders. Their endorsements can lend credibility to your campaign.[22]

---

19 M. Hite, "What to Do after Your School Bond Election—However It Went," SchoolCEO, 2023, www.schoolceo.com/a/what-to-do-after-your-school-bond-election-however-it-went.

20 Ibid.

21 K12 Insight, *School Bond Campaigns,* 2018, https://www.k12insight.com/news/school-bond-campaigns/.

22 M. Hite, "What to Do after Your School Bond Election—However It Went," SchoolCEO, 2023, www.schoolceo.com/a/what-to-do-after-your-school-bond-election-however-it-went.

Community Events

Host community events, town halls, and informational sessions to engage with voters directly. These events provide an opportunity for questions and discussions.[23]

Media Relations

Establish relationships with local media outlets. Write press releases, op-eds, and letters to the editor to keep the bond issue in the news. Consider editorial board meetings to secure newspaper endorsements.[24]

Grassroots Campaigning

Mobilize volunteers to go door to door, make phone calls, and distribute campaign materials. Personal interactions can be very persuasive.[25]

Storytelling and Testimonials

Share stories and testimonials from students, parents, and teachers who have benefited from previous bond measures or who will benefit from the proposed bond.[26]

Transparency and Accountability

Be transparent about how the bond funds will be used and establish mechanisms for oversight and accountability. Show that you are a responsible steward of taxpayer dollars.[27]

---

23 Ibid.

24 Ibid.

25 Ibid.

26 Ibid.

27 Ibid.

Partnerships

Seek endorsements and support from local organizations, chambers of commerce, and advocacy groups that align with the goals of the bond.[28]

Targeted Messaging

Tailor your messages to specific demographics within your community. Different groups may have varying concerns or priorities.[29]

Legal Compliance

Ensure that your campaign complies with all campaign finance and election laws. This includes disclosing campaign contributions and expenditures.[30]

Get Out the Vote (GOTV)

In the final days leading up to the election, focus on getting supporters to the polls. Use phone banks, canvassing, and targeted messaging to remind people to vote.[31]

Postelection Communication

Regardless of the outcome, maintain communication with the community. If the bond passes, provide updates on progress. If it fails, solicit feedback and consider adjustments for the future.[32]

Remember that building trust and demonstrating the bond's benefits to the community are key to a successful branding strategy for passing a school bond in California or any other location. Tailor your

---

28 Ibid.
29 Ibid.
30 Ibid.
31 Ibid.
32 Ibid.

approach to your specific community's needs and concerns to increase your chances of success.[33]

Communicating Better

What I really love about what ChatGPT produced is that it affirms everything we have written in this book so far from branding to networking to Liberatory Design, street data, and community schools.

K12 Insight surveyed district leaders who successfully passed bonds. Here are five lessons they learned (you'll see it mirrors what ChatGPT produced as well). Their professional tip was that "it's all about how you communicate your vision":

1. Listen to community partners.
2. Build your proposal around community needs.
3. Personalize your message for different audiences.
4. Use multiple channels of communication.
5. Engage your community in a "two-way" conversation.[34]

According to Athena Vadnais, APR, "Direct mail is good for getting information into the hands of voters who don't have a daily connection with your schools. Social media is an easy and cost-effective way to communicate with people. Face-to-face communication is the most time-consuming, but it's also the most effective way to communicate. Go where the voters are. Go to civic club meetings. Go to your local diner, where retirees hang out in the mornings—and share information about your bond with them."[35]

Whether it is school bonds or budgets, sites and districts could all do a better job of communicating where and how money is spent or will be spent and how that is linked to vision, mission, and values.

---

33 Ibid.

34 K12 Insight, *School Bond Campaigns,* 2018, https://www.k12insight.com/news/school-bond-campaigns/.

35 Ibid.

Even more importantly, they should show how it will be used to support scholars and staff.

TIPS, STRATEGIES, AND REFLECTIONS

- What other ideas do you have about branding and school bonds?

Please share your reflections using the #EdBranding hashtag and visit EdBranding.net for more ideas on intentional educational branding to successfully pass a school bond.

THE 50,000-FOOT VIEW

PUBLIC EDUCATION, BRANDING, AND OUR DEMOCRACY

Stay Empowered

Renae

Dave Burgess called sharing the positives about what we are doing in public education our "moral imperative." That's because, as a part of the culture wars, there is a group within the United States that is trying to erode the promise and power of public education.[36] Everyone who believes in the power of public education to strengthen and protect our democracy must do their part to share the powerful success stories of public education. We all must do our part to counter the extreme narratives created by those who seek to destroy public education and our democracy. We cannot allow a death by a thousand cuts. We have to do our part to be sure the public understands how incredible and necessary our public schools are.

---

36 J. Schneider and J. Berkshire, *A Wolf at the Schoolhouse Door: The Dismantling of Public Education and the Future of School* (New York: The New Press, 2020).

On the *Voices of Excellence Podcast* hosted by Dr. Michael Conner, I was asked which three words I would end the episode with; I will use the same three to conclude here.

Love

US Army Major General John H. Stanford is quoted in Kouzes and Posner's seminal work *The Leadership Challenge* as saying, "The secret to success is to stay in love." Love the people and love the work. Stay in love with achieving excellence and equity.

Courage

First we need love, and second we need courage. We need courage to truly live by our core values. Core values are easy to live by when they're convenient. There are points (like when a local district kicked California State Superintendent of Public Instruction Tony Thurmond out of their board meeting) that I feel appalled, angry, and heartbroken about the attacks on public education. Then I remember the courage it took to desegregate schools. We know we have de facto segregation and real segregation in parts of the South—and still, think of all the courage it took to fight for civil rights. People with great courage lost their lives. When I ground myself back in the history of courage, then I am not appalled, angry, or heartbroken. I feel resolute in my call to courageous transformational leadership.

Significance

Keep living in your purpose and significance, keep doing this hard work, this work based in love and courage, to create greater excellence and equity for our historically excluded scholars.

One More Word: Freedom

I want to end with one of my favorite Martin Luther King Jr. quotes: "Freedom is never voluntarily given by the oppressor; it must be demanded by the oppressed." Our scholars deserve our love, courage, and significance to demand equity, access, and opportunity; empower them to demand it.

Storytelling for Democracy

Lynette

Storytelling in education is not a new concept; however, its significance has been magnified in the digital age. Stories have the power to connect, engage, and inspire. In the context of public education, storytelling becomes a tool for educators and institutions to communicate their values, missions, and achievements. It goes beyond relaying facts and figures. It's about creating a narrative that resonates with students, parents, and the community at large. This narrative is crucial in shaping the brand of educational institutions—a brand that reflects their commitment to nurturing informed, thoughtful, and participative members of society.

Social media platforms offer an unprecedented opportunity to amplify these stories. In a time when information is abundantly accessible and attention spans are probably at the shortest they've ever been, social media provides a direct and engaging way to reach a diverse audience. We can leverage these platforms to showcase successes, share educational resources, and foster a sense of community. More importantly, social media can be a democratic space where students, educators, and parents can engage in dialogues, exchange ideas, and participate in the educational process. This interaction not only enhances the learning experience but also fosters a sense of ownership and involvement in the democratic process.

The integration of storytelling and social media in public education is more than a strategic approach to branding; it's a fundamental
component in fostering a democratic spirit. By effectively telling their
stories and engaging with the community on social media, educational
institutions can reinforce the values of democracy—participation,
inclusivity, and informed decision-making. We hope educators and
administrators embrace these tools, not just to enhance the educational
experience, but to contribute to the larger goal of sustaining and enrich-
ing our democracy. In today's fast-paced and digitally interconnected
world, the role of public education extends beyond the traditional con-
fines of classrooms and textbooks. It's about shaping the future of our
democracy by creating informed, engaged, and responsible citizens.

We hope this book empowers you to brand boldly and courageously
with love. Your voice and the voice of your scholars, staff, caregivers/
families, and community deserve to be heard.

Please share your reflections using the #EdBranding hashtag and
visit EdBranding.net for more ideas on how you can do your part
to save public education and our democracy by continuing to
share the positive narratives.

REFERENCES

Anaissie, T., V. Cary, D. Clifford, T. Malarkey, and S. Wise. *Liberatory Design.* 2021. http://www.liberatorydesign.com.

Botwin, A. "Power vs Influence: How It Can Make or Break Your Organization." SPC Consulting. October 3, 2022. https://www.strategypeopleculture.com/blog/power-vs-influence/.

Bryant, R., J. Jackson, V. Mayfield, and J. Root. "A Communications Plan to Effectively Communicate a Single Story." Capstone project, AASA USC Urban Superintendents Academy, 2019.

Burgess, D. *Teach Like a Pirate: Increase Student Engagement, Boost Your Creativity, and Transform Your Life as an Educator.* San Diego, CA: Dave Burgess Consulting, Inc, 2012.

Couros, G. *The Innovator's Mindset.* San Diego, CA: Dave Burgess Consulting, Inc., 2015.

Covey, S. M. R., and R. Merrill. *The Speed of Trust: The One Thing That Changes Everything.* New York: Free Press, 2008.

Creasman, B., B. Futrell, and T. Rubin. *ConnectEd Leaders.* Lanham, MD: Rowman & Littlefield, 2019.

Creed, G., and K. Muench. *R.E.D Marketing: The Three Ingredients of Leading Brands.* New York: HarperCollins, 2021.

Fagen, Friedman, and Fulfrost LLP. Communications. ACSA Superintendents Academy. Whittier, CA: Whittier City School District Office, January 20, 2018.

Fitzpatrick, D., A. Fox, and B. Weinstein. *The AI Classroom: The Ultimate Guide to Artificial Intelligence in Education.* Beechgrove, IN: TeacherGoals Publishing, 2023.

Hite, M. "What to Do after Your School Bond Election—However It Went." SchoolCEO. 2023. www.schoolceo.com/a/what-to-do-after-your-school-bond-election-however-it-went.

K12 Insight. *School Bond Campaigns.* 2018. https://www.k12insight.com/news/school-bond-campaigns/.

Martin, T. *Be REAL: Educate from the Heart.* San Diego, CA: Dave Burgess Consulting, Inc., 2018.

Miller, M. *AI for Educators: Learning Strategies, Teacher Efficiencies, and a Vision for an Artificial Intelligence Future*. San Diego, CA: Ditch That Textbook, 2023.

Nesloney, T., and A. Welcome, *Kids Deserve It: Pushing Boundaries and Challenging Conventional Thinking.* San Diego, CA: Dave Burgess Consulting, Inc., 2016.

Rubin, T. "Define before Being Defined!" National Conference on Education. Symposium conducted at the conference of the AASA The School Superintendents Association, Los Angeles, CA, February 2019.

Ruiz, M., and N. Wilton. *The Four Agreements: A Practical Guide to Personal Freedom*. San Rafael, CA: Amber-Allen, 2012.

Safir, S., and J. Dugan. *Street Data: A Next Generation Model for Equity, Pedagogy, and School Transformation*. Thousand Oaks, CA: Corwin, 2021.

Schneider, J., and J. Berkshire. *A Wolf at the Schoolhouse Door: The Dismantling of Public Education and the Future of School*. New York: The New Press, 2020.

Sheninger, E. *Digital Leadership*. Thousand Oaks, CA: Corwin, 2014.

Sheninger, E., and T. Rubin. *BrandED*. San Francisco, CA: Jossey-Bass, 2017.

Sinanis, T., and J. Sanfelippo. *The Power of Branding: Telling Your School's Story*. Thousand Oaks, CA: Corwin, 2015.

Stanford, L. "What 2024 Will Bring for K12 Policy: 5 Issues to Watch." Edweek. December 29, 2023. https://www.edweek.org/policy-politics/what-2024-will-bring-for-k-12-policy-5-issues-to-watch/2023/12.

University of the People. "Teachers and Social Media: The Online Pros and Cons." December 20, 2022. https://www.uopeople.edu/blog/teachers-and-social-media/.

ACKNOWLEDGMENTS

Lynette White

To my awesome family: I do all I can to make you proud, because you each continue to fill me with pride daily. I'm blessed to get to be called Mom by the three best kids there are. Kaia, Jaylen, and Isabella—love you to the moon and back and hope you see that YES YOU CAN! Drew—thank you for being a supportive partner. Without you this wouldn't be possible. Mom—this is my thank-you for your hard work and instilling in me the strength to be myself. Also, you were right about like 99 percent of everything. Ma siempre me dijiste que podía hacerlo. Lo hice y fue sólo por el amor incondicional que me diste todos los días. Te quiero mucho.

To my mentors: This book is dedicated to each of you who have taught, supported, and loved me as I learn and grow to be a better leader each day. I am grateful to have crossed paths with you all and blessed to get to call each of you my friend: Dr. Stefanie Phillips, Jerry Almendarez, Dr. Lorraine Perez, Dr. Nyree Clark, Jessica Gomez, Dr. Kerri Braun, Laura Castro, Terrence Davis, and the many more who took the time to see something in me that I never saw myself.

To my coauthor: Dr. Renae Bryant! Without you, this would have never been. You are an amazing human who I am blessed to share a book with and incredibly proud to now call you friend as well. Forever grateful.

Renae Bryant

Dave Burgess, Tara Martin, Adam Welcome, and Sal Borriello—thank you for believing in us and the power of this book to make a positive impact on the education community and our democracy.

To my mother, Sharon Foster—thank you for realizing the dream of taking your little red wagon to California. Our journeys were always connected and will continue to be. I always knew you believed in me, supported me, and prayed for me. The sacrifices you made in this lifetime helped me to become the person I was meant to be. I love you and cherish our conversations and time spent together. You are a wonderful example of an independent woman. I am proud of you and the courage you show in your journey. Thank you for all you did for me. I am proud to be your daughter. Thank you for all you do for all those around you and the glory you give to God.

To my best friend, Jared Schweitzer—thank you for your friendship and support. Through each journey, you keep the furry children fed and alive. I appreciate you.

To the AUHSD, WSD, and CNUSD scholars, colleagues, families, and community partners (past and present)—thank you for allowing me to learn and lead beside you while I live out my purpose and passion of collaboratively making a positive difference through public education.

To my #SisterCircleLWF—Heidi Baker, Cynthia Covarrubias, Dr. Kimberly MacKinney, Margie Cuizon-Armelino, Dr. Stacie Stanley, Dr. Lori Gonzalez, Michelle Mower, and Dr. Patricia Trejo—thank you for your friendship, sisterhood, and support. I love you, sisters.

To my #SisterCircleE3—Dr. Benisha Carr, Dr. Donna Hunter, Dr. Marguerite Williams, Dr. Kimberley MacKinney, Dr. Terry Walker, and Dr. Talisa Sullivan—thank you for being my original sister circle; your friendship, sisterhood, and support. I love you, sisters.

To my #SisterCircleCABERiverside—Mary Helen Ybarra, Addie Ruiz, Susana Quintero, Aracely (Nelly) Ceja, Elizabeth Maciel, Esther Garcia, Veronica Perez, Patricia Thetford, Jan Gustafson-Corea, and Vienessa Lopez—thank you for your advocacy for our plurilingual scholars, their families, and the staff who serve them. Thank you for dedicating your time and energy to increasing plurilingualism and equity for all. Thank you for your friendship, sisterhood, and support. I love you, sisters.

To all of the mentors and sponsors—I stand on the shoulders of giants. I can only hope to make half of the positive impact you have.

To my coauthor and #EdBranding copodcaster, Lynette White—thank you for replying to my text and taking that Zoom meeting with me to discuss an idea about writing a book together. I am so fortunate that you said yes and to be on this journey with you. I am forever grateful to Jerry Almendarez for originally connecting us. You are a talented, compassionate, and brilliant friend, now sister. Do I see a #SisterCircleEB coming on? Maybe! I love you and your incredible family. The sky's the limit for all of you. I am excited to see where this journey takes us!

ABOUT THE AUTHORS

Lynette White

Lynette White's career in education spans fourteen years and three school districts. She is currently the district and community relations coordinator for Banning USD. Prior to that, Lynette served as the communications specialist for Colton Joint Unified School District and previously worked in a variety of roles at Santa Ana USD for twelve and a half years, completing her career with SAUSD as the executive assistant to the superintendent of schools.

Ms. White is an edu-influencer who has presented statewide on the importance of telling your story and maximizing your efforts on social media to brand yourself as a leader and brand your organization as well as the importance of developing a valuable professional learning network. Lynette is the cohost of the *Ed Branding Podcast*, whose audience spans fifty states and eighteen countries. The podcast works to empower people to share their story while also sharing leadership strategies. Lynette is the owner of a communications consulting company, Lynette White Social, LLC, and copartner of ConnectED. Both companies work with organizations to amplify their stories.

Lynette holds her Bachelor of Arts in Communications with an emphasis on New Media from Southern New Hampshire University and will be completing her Master of Arts in Communications with an emphasis on Education from Grand Canyon University in Spring 2024. Lynette is the assistant regional chair for Orange County/Inland Empire for the California School Public Relations Association. She was recently recognized as a 2023 Rising Star for the California School Public Relations Association as well as being recognized with the 2023 MOSAIC Inclusivity Excellence Award.

Dr. Renae Bryant

Dr. Renae Bryant serves as the director of plurilingual services at Anaheim Union High School District (AUHSD) in Anaheim, California, where she works collaboratively with scholars, staff, families, and community to build systems and processes to increase student access, opportunity, equity, and success through the plurilingual, world languages, and Spanish and Vietnamese dual language immersion (DLI) programs. Dr. Bryant led teams to successfully move AUHSD out of ATSI.

Previously at Westminster School District, Renae led a team to implement the first Vietnamese DLI program in California, which was awarded the California School Board Associations Golden Bell in 2017, and at AUHSD the first secondary Vietnamese DLI program in the United States. At AUHSD she has nominated and earned California School Board Association Golden Bell Awards in her department for: 2019 AUHSD Dual Language Immersion Programs, 2019 AUHSD Summer Language Academy, and 2022 AUHSD Saturday Language Academy. She is a successful grant writer with over $1 million in professional learning grants written.

She is the founder and facilitator of the Leadership Book Chat and leads national book studies featuring expert speakers leading the learning on such books as: *Leading while Female, How to Be an Antiracist, The New Jim Crow, Ready for Anything, How Women Rise, Beyond Conversations about Race, The Unfinished Leader, Evolving Learner, She Leads, Leading Change through the Lens of Cultural Proficiency*, and *Lead with Collaboration*. She is the past president of the California Association of Bilingual Education (CABE) Riverside Chapter, serves as the Association of California School Administrators (ACSA) Region 17 president elect of public relations, and is the chair of the ACSA Urban Education Committee. In the summer, she serves as an adjunct professor at CSUF for the EdD Program, where she teaches the Organizational Theory and Instructional Challenges course.

With over twenty years in education, Renae has served as a district, site, and teacher leader, administrator, coach, and started bilingual special education instructional assistant. She is the contributing author to *Radically Inclusive Teaching for Emergent Plurilingual Newcomers: Braving Up* and the author of *Teacher Leader Behaviors: A Quantitative Study of a Teacher Leader Development Academy and Teacher Leaders' Five Practices of Exemplary Leadership Behaviors* (ProQuest). She cohosts *The Ed Branding Podcast*.

Dr. Bryant earned her Doctorate in Organizational Leadership at the University of La Verne in 2017 and completed AASA/USC Urban

Superintendents Academy, Stanford EdLEADers Program and is currently in the Azusa Pacific University Next Generation Superintendents Academy. She was named 2019 ACSA Region 17 Valuing Diversity Administrator of the Year, 2022 MOSAIC Inclusivity Awardee, and in 2023 was honored with two Women of Distinction Awards, one by 34th Senate District Senator Thomas J. Umberg and one by 67th Assembly District Assemblywoman Sharon Quirk-Silva. Renae was named the 2024 California Association for Bilingual Education (CABE) District Administrator of the Year.

INVITE RENAE AND LYNETTE TO SPEAK AT YOUR NEXT EVENT

Lynette has been delivering exciting presentations and professional development sessions with districts for years. Additionally, Lynette consults with districts on social media marketing, brand ambassador programs, and much more! Connect with her at:

- lynettewhitesocial@gmail.com
- lynettewhite.com
- edbranding.net

Renae has been collaborating with educators to build capacity through keynote presentations and professional learning opportunities for over a decade. Renae delivers keynotes and consults on educational branding, systems work in organizations, leadership, increasing access, equity, and success for our most at-promise scholars, plurilingualism, translanguaging, newcomers, dual language immersion, Liberatory Design, sister circles, and more.

- renae.bryant@laverne.edu
- renaebryant.com

- edbranding.net
- Twitter (X): @DrRenaeBryant
- IG: @DrRenaeBryant
- LI: Renae Bryant, Ed.D.
- FB: Renae Bryant

MORE FROM

Since 2012, DBCI has published books that inspire and equip educators to be their best. For more information on our titles or to purchase bulk orders for your school, district, or book study, visit DaveBurgessConsulting.com/DBCIbooks.

The Like a PIRATE™ Series

Teach Like a PIRATE by Dave Burgess
eXPlore Like a PIRATE by Michael Matera
Learn Like a PIRATE by Paul Solarz
Plan Like a PIRATE by Dawn M. Harris
Play Like a PIRATE by Quinn Rollins
Run Like a PIRATE by Adam Welcome
Tech Like a PIRATE by Matt Miller

The Lead Like a PIRATE™ Series

Lead Like a PIRATE by Shelley Burgess and Beth Houf
Balance Like a PIRATE by Jessica Cabeen, Jessica Johnson, and Sarah Johnson
Lead beyond Your Title by Nili Bartley
Lead with Appreciation by Amber Teamann and Melinda Miller
Lead with Collaboration by Allyson Apsey and Jessica Gomez

Lead with Culture by Jay Billy
Lead with Instructional Rounds by Vicki Wilson
Lead with Literacy by Mandy Ellis
She Leads by Dr. Rachael George and Majalise W. Tolan

The EduProtocol Field Guide Series

Deploying EduProtocols by Kim Voge, with Jon Corippo and
　　Marlena Hebern
The EduProtocol Field Guide by Marlena Hebern and Jon Corippo
The EduProtocol Field Guide: Book 2 by Marlena Hebern and
　　Jon Corippo
The EduProtocol Field Guide: Math Edition by Lisa Nowakowski
　　and Jeremiah Ruesch
The EduProtocol Field Guide: Primary Edition by Benjamin
　　Cogswell and Jennifer Dean
The EduProtocol Field Guide: Social Studies Edition by Dr. Scott M.
　　Petri and Adam Moler

Leadership & School Culture

Beyond the Surface of Restorative Practices by Marisol Rerucha
Change the Narrative by Henry J. Turner and Kathy Lopes
Choosing to See by Pamela Seda and Kyndall Brown
Culturize by Jimmy Casas
Discipline Win by Andy Jacks
Educate Me! by Dr. Shree Walker with Micheal D. Ison
Escaping the School Leader's Dunk Tank by Rebecca Coda and
　　Rick Jetter
Fight Song by Kim Bearden
From Teacher to Leader by Starr Sackstein
If the Dance Floor Is Empty, Change the Song by Joe Clark
The Innovator's Mindset by George Couros
It's OK to Say "They" by Christy Whittlesey
Kids Deserve It! by Todd Nesloney and Adam Welcome
Leading the Whole Teacher by Allyson Apsey
Let Them Speak by Rebecca Coda and Rick Jetter

The Limitless School by Abe Hege and Adam Dovico
Live Your Excellence by Jimmy Casas
Next-Level Teaching by Jonathan Alsheimer
The Pepper Effect by Sean Gaillard
Principaled by Kate Barker, Kourtney Ferrua, and Rachael George
The Principled Principal by Jeffrey Zoul and Anthony McConnell
Relentless by Hamish Brewer
The Secret Solution by Todd Whitaker, Sam Miller, and
     Ryan Donlan
Start. Right. Now. by Todd Whitaker, Jeffrey Zoul, and Jimmy Casas
Stop. Right. Now. by Jimmy Casas and Jeffrey Zoul
Teachers Deserve It by Rae Hughart and Adam Welcome
Teach Your Class Off by CJ Reynolds
They Call Me "Mr. De" by Frank DeAngelis
Thrive through the Five by Jill M. Siler
Unmapped Potential by Julie Hasson and Missy Lennard
When Kids Lead by Todd Nesloney and Adam Dovico
Word Shift by Joy Kirr
Your School Rocks by Ryan McLane and Eric Lowe

Technology & Tools

50 Things to Go Further with Google Classroom by Alice Keeler
     and Libbi Miller
50 Things You Can Do with Google Classroom by Alice Keeler and
     Libbi Miller
50 Ways to Engage Students with Google Apps by Alice Keeler and
     Heather Lyon
140 Twitter Tips for Educators by Brad Currie, Billy Krakower, and
     Scott Rocco
Block Breaker by Brian Aspinall
Building Blocks for Tiny Techies by Jamila "Mia" Leonard
Code Breaker by Brian Aspinall
The Complete EdTech Coach by Katherine Goyette and
     Adam Juarez
Control Alt Achieve by Eric Curts
The Esports Education Playbook by Chris Aviles, Steve Isaacs,
     Christine Lion-Bailey, and Jesse Lubinsky

Google Apps for Littles by Christine Pinto and Alice Keeler

Master the Media by Julie Smith

Raising Digital Leaders by Jennifer Casa-Todd

Reality Bytes by Christine Lion-Bailey, Jesse Lubinsky, and Micah
    Shippee, PhD

Sail the 7 Cs with Microsoft Education by Becky Keene and
    Kathi Kersznowski

Shake Up Learning by Kasey Bell

Social LEADia by Jennifer Casa-Todd

Stepping Up to Google Classroom by Alice Keeler and
    Kimberly Mattina

Teaching Math with Google Apps by Alice Keeler and
    Diana Herrington

Teaching with Google Jamboard by Alice Keeler and
    Kimberly Mattina

Teachingland by Amanda Fox and Mary Ellen Weeks

Teaching Methods & Materials

All 4s and 5s by Andrew Sharos

Boredom Busters by Katie Powell

The Classroom Chef by John Stevens and Matt Vaudrey

The Collaborative Classroom by Trevor Muir

Copyrighteous by Diana Gill

CREATE by Bethany J. Petty

Ditch That Homework by Matt Miller and Alice Keeler

Ditch That Textbook by Matt Miller

Don't Ditch That Tech by Matt Miller, Nate Ridgway, and
    Angelia Ridgway

EDrenaline Rush by John Meehan

Educated by Design by Michael Cohen, The Tech Rabbi

Empowered to Choose: A Practical Guide to Personalized Learning
    by Andrew Easton

Expedition Science by Becky Schnekser

Frustration Busters by Katie Powell

Fully Engaged by Michael Matera and John Meehan

Game On? Brain On! by Lindsay Portnoy, PhD

Guided Math AMPED by Reagan Tunstall

Happy & Resilient by Roni Habib

Innovating Play by Jessica LaBar-Twomy and Christine Pinto

Instant Relevance by Denis Sheeran

Instructional Coaching Connection by Nathan Lang-Raad

Keeping the Wonder by Jenna Copper, Ashley Bible, Abby Gross, and Staci Lamb

LAUNCH by John Spencer and A.J. Juliani

Learning in the Zone by Dr. Sonny Magana

Lights, Cameras, TEACH! by Kevin J. Butler

Make Learning MAGICAL by Tisha Richmond

Pass the Baton by Kathryn Finch and Theresa Hoover

Project-Based Learning Anywhere by Lori Elliott

Pure Genius by Don Wettrick

The Revolution by Darren Ellwein and Derek McCoy

The Science Box by Kim Adsit and Adam Peterson

Shift This! by Joy Kirr

Skyrocket Your Teacher Coaching by Michael Cary Sonbert

Spark Learning by Ramsey Musallam

Sparks in the Dark by Travis Crowder and Todd Nesloney

Table Talk Math by John Stevens

Teachables by Cheryl Abla and Lisa Maxfield

Unpack Your Impact by Naomi O'Brien and LaNesha Tabb

The Wild Card by Hope and Wade King

Writefully Empowered by Jacob Chastain

The Writing on the Classroom Wall by Steve Wyborney

You Are Poetry by Mike Johnston

You'll Never Guess What I'm Saying by Naomi O'Brien

You'll Never Guess What I'm Thinking About by Naomi O'Brien

Inspiration, Professional Growth & Personal Development

Be REAL by Tara Martin

Be the One for Kids by Ryan Sheehy

The Coach ADVenture by Amy Illingworth

Creatively Productive by Lisa Johnson

Educational Eye Exam by Alicia Ray

The EduNinja Mindset by Jennifer Burdis

Empower Our Girls by Lynmara Colón and Adam Welcome
Finding Lifelines by Andrew Grieve and Andrew Sharos
The Four O'Clock Faculty by Rich Czyz
How Much Water Do We Have? by Pete and Kris Nunweiler
P Is for Pirate by Dave and Shelley Burgess
PheMOMenal Teacher by Annick Rauch
A Passion for Kindness by Tamara Letter
The Path to Serendipity by Allyson Apsey
Recipes for Resilience by Robert A. Martinez
Rogue Leader by Rich Czyz
Sanctuaries by Dan Tricarico
Saving Sycamore by Molly B. Hudgens
The Secret Sauce by Rich Czyz
Shattering the Perfect Teacher Myth by Aaron Hogan
Stories from Webb by Todd Nesloney
Talk to Me by Kim Bearden
Teach Better by Chad Ostrowski, Tiffany Ott, Rae Hughart, and
    Jeff Gargas
Teach Me, Teacher by Jacob Chastain
Teach, Play, Learn! by Adam Peterson
The Teachers of Oz by Herbie Raad and Nathan Lang-Raad
TeamMakers by Laura Robb and Evan Robb
Through the Lens of Serendipity by Allyson Apsey
Write Here and Now by Dan Tricarico
The Zen Teacher by Dan Tricarico

Children's Books

The Adventures of Little Mickey by Mickey Smith Jr.
Alpert by LaNesha Tabb
Alpert & Friends by LaNesha Tabb
Beyond Us by Aaron Polansky
Cannonball In by Tara Martin
Dolphins in Trees by Aaron Polansky
Dragon Smart by Tisha and Tommy Richmond
I Can Achieve Anything by MoNique Waters
I Want to Be a Lot by Ashley Savage

The Magic of Wonder by Jenna Copper, Ashley Bible, Abby Gross, and Staci Lamb

Micah's Big Question by Naomi O'Brien

The Princes of Serendip by Allyson Apsey

Ride with Emilio by Richard Nares

A Teacher's Top Secret Confidential by LaNesha Tabb

A Teacher's Top Secret: Mission Accomplished by LaNesha Tabb

The Wild Card Kids by Hope and Wade King

Zom-Be a Design Thinker by Amanda Fox

www.ingramcontent.com/pod-product-compliance
Lightning Source LLC
Jackson TN
JSHW012236230525
84764JS00005B/16